Ketogenic Diet Reci... Minutes or Le...

Beginner's Weight Loss Keto Cookbook Guide

By Sydney Foster

© 2017

Table of Content

Contents

Introduction 7

What Is the Ketogenic Diet? 9

   Basic Types 9

   Some Keto Benefits 10

Getting Started 13

What to Buy: 13

   Foods to Avoid 17

Your One Week Meal Plan 17

   Sunday 17

   Monday 18

   Tuesday 18

   Wednesday 19

   Thursday 19

   Friday 20

   Saturday 20

Starting with Breakfast 21

   Tropical Delight 21

   Keto MacMuffin 22

   Feta & Spinach Omelet 23

   Chocolate Pancakes 24

   Spicy Eggs & Cheese Hash 25

   Salmon Breakfast Bombs 26

   Pesto Mug Muffin 27

   Keto Hash Browns 28

Sausage Breakfast 29

Green Machine Smoothie 30

Keto French Toast 31

Chocolate & Blackberry Smoothie 32

Spinach Scrambled Eggs 32

Sausage & Feta Omelet 33

Cheddar & Chive Omelet 34

Banana & Blueberry Bread Smoothie 35

Eggs in Purgatory 36

Cream Cheese & Salmon Bites 37

Lunch Recipes 39

Easy Pork Salad 39

Mug Melt 40

Mug Lasagna 41

Simple Mixed Green Salad 42

Easy Keto Soup 42

Easy Tuna Salad 43

Egg & Avocado Salad 44

Mackerel Salad 45

Chive & Cheddar Mug Cake 47

Egg Drop Soup 47

Jalapeno Mug Cake 48

Spinach & Goat Cheese Salad 49

Bacon & Avocado Salad 50

Mushroom & Cheese Mug 51

BLT Lettuce Wrap 52

Dinner Recipes 55

Zoodle Alfredo 55

Thai Inspired Pork Salad 56

Fried Fish 57

Pesto Sea Bass 58

Keto Pizza 59

Pizza Frittata 61

Spicy Prawn Rolls 62

Curried Chicken Rolls 63

Lemon & Thyme Chicken 64

Bunless BBQ Burgers 65

Meatballs on a Stick 66

Spinach & Scallops 67

Perfect Pork Chops 69

Stuffed Avocado with Cajun Chicken 70

Cheesy "Risotto" 71

Egg Stuffed Avocado 72

Veggie Burgers 73

Prawn Stir Fry 74

Easy Chicken Stir Fry 76

Spiced Meatballs 77

Side Dishes 79

Garlic Broccoli 79

Summer Salsa 80

Guacamole 81

Cheese Sauce 82

Lemon Green Beans 83

Keto Mac & Cheese 83

Asian Broccoli Salad 84

Crispy Kale Sprouts 85

Sugar Snap Peas with Bacon 86

Red Pepper Spinach Salad 87

Snack Recipes 89

Fried Cheese 89

Pesto Bombs 90

Cheesecake Dip 90

Zucchini Rolls 91

Easy Parmesan Crisps 92

Garlic Fried Zucchini 93

Dessert Recipes 95

Brownie Mug Cake 95

Cinnamon Mug Cake 96

Chocolate Frostino 97

Pumpkin Spice Latte 97

Turmeric Iced Latte 98

Chocolate Chip Cookies 99

Mint & Chocolate Smoothie 100

Hot Spiced Mocha 101

Chocolate Mug 101

Berry Sauce & Pancake 103

Red Velvet Mug 104

Eggnog Mug Cake 106

Strawberry Milkshake 106

Vanilla Mug Cake 107

Orange Chocolate Chia Pudding 108

Conclusion 110

Introduction

Many people try diet after diet to try to find what works for them, and often they gain the weight back right after they lose it. Others view the word diet as something they must suffer through, deal with the inadequate food and hunger pains, and give up the food they love. The ketogenic diet is different, and you won't have to go hungry just because you have to limit your carbs. Say goodbye to hunger pangs and hello to the body and lifestyle that you want.

With the ketogenic diet, you're making a lifestyle choice. With moderate exercise and a diet that keeps you full, you'll be able to gain control of your weight and your health. In this book you'll find all of the recipes you need out start your ketogenic diet today despite a busy day to day life, a week long meal plan to get you started, and even knowledge of what food to stock up on and what to avoid. With quick and easy recipes, there's nothing to hold you back from shedding those extra pounds and eating right!

What Is the Ketogenic Diet?

To understand the ketogenic diet and why it works, you need to understand where the word keto is derived from. It's derived from a metabolic process that's called ketosis where the body starts to produce ketones. The aim of this diet is lowering your intake of carbohydrates while you increase your intake of fat. This is a high-fat, low carb diet which is often just referred to as a low carb diet. When your body takes in a large amount of carbs it produces glucose and insulin will rise to a peak. Glucose can then be converted into energy, and your body is actually used to relying on that energy for daily activities. Insulin will help to regulate the level of glucose in your blood stream, and if your glucose rises to high your insulin will work to lower it.

Since your body is used to storing fat and using glucose as its energy, it will not use the stored fat until the amount of glucose your body has to burn as energy is lowered. So as long as you stay on a high carb diet, your fat levels won't go down. This is where you need the keto diet. You'll keep your body from the carbs it's used to having, which will force it into a state of ketosis. During this process it'll release ketones, encouraging your body to use stored fat to supply you with the energy you need to function.

Basic Types

There are three types of ketogenic diet, and this book caters to the standard ketogenic diet.

- **Standard:** This diet consists of a low car band high fat intake with moderate protein. Usually it's around 75% fat, 5% carbs and about 20% protein. This diet is good for the average person that is looking to stay in ketosis and lose weight. A high protein ketogenic diet is a modified standard diet, which just has 35% protein, 5% carbs and 60% fats. This is better for someone who works out often or is an athlete.

- **Targeted:** The targeted ketogenic diet will give you the freedom to have more carbs right before a heavy workout. It's important to know that the targeted diet should not be used for people who aren't working out regularly. If you use a targeted ketogenic diet for mild exercise or infrequent exercise, you can end up gaining the weight you lose back or not lose weight at all.
- **Cyclical:** The cyclical ketogenic diet has days where you are on the diet, staying in ketosis and then days that you take off. This is not good for the standard person, but it can be sued if the alternative is infrequent use of the diet. Most people go with five days on the ketogenic diet and five days off of it. However, other people will use it with a full week on the ketogenic diet and then a cheat day before going back on.

Some Keto Benefits

Now that you know what the ketogenic diet is, you may be wondering if it has any benefits besides weight loss. The answer is yes, and you'll find those benefits below.

- **Managed Hunger:** If you're on a diet or not, you'll find that it can be hard to manage hunger. Any other diet would often have you hungry the majority of the time, as you're restricting your intake of food. This is not the case with the ketogenic diet. Hunger is the main reason that diets are not followed, and it can be a nightmare for all involved. You'll also experienced reduced cravings on the ketogenic diet, which will help you to keep from cheating. Calorie counting is not necessary with this diet so long as you stay under twenty net carbs a day.
- **Easy Weight Maintenance:** It can be hard to maintain your desired weight if you're always off and on a diet again. However, with just moderate exercise you can maintain your weight by continuing to follow this diet. The keto diet turns your body into a fat burning machine, and without hunger it can be easy to switch to the ketogenic lifestyle.

- **Quick Exercise Recovery:** Exercise is an important tool in weight loss, and it's necessary to tone your body. Though, even though weight loss is helped along by exercise, it can be difficult to stick to exercise when you have to deal with strains and aching muscles. The ketogenic diet can help with this too! Your body's inflammation is one of the key reasons that your body aches after a workout, and the ketogenic diet will systematically help to take care of that inflammation as a result of the lower carbs.
- **Regulates Your Insulin:** Your body needs insulin to use glucose and regulate blood sugar. Your insulin acts as the messenger to make your cells open and use the glucose as the energy source. On a high carb diet, you'll have various insulin spikes which can leave your blood sugar levels out of control. However, with ketosis your body experiences lowered levels of blood sugar because you consume less carbs. This will keep your insulin from spiking as well.
- **Improved Cholesterol:** Good cholesterol reacts well to the keto diet, and the keto diet will help to lower your cholesterol. However, don't expect this benefit to show up overnight. It takes time for the keto diet to work on your cholesterol levels, especially if they were already bad.
- **Energizes You:** The ketogenic diet will energize you too! Ketones are a source of energy that's more reliable, and therefore you'll notice improved energy throughout the day. Even if you experience chronic fatigue, you'll feel better with the keto diet.
- **Enhanced Mood & Clarity:** Ketones can also help to stabilize and enhance your moods as well as provide more clear thought. This is because they stabilize neurotransmitters such as serotonin and dopamine.
- **Better Digestion:** The keto diet is easier on your digestive system. This is due to the reduced grain and sugar consumption. It will also help to relieve bloating for the same reason.

Getting Started

If you've decided to take the plunge into the ketogenic lifestyle, you may be at a loss at how to start. Getting your pantry started is the first place to start, but this can be easier said than done.

What to Buy:

Here is a list of what you should buy in order to stock your kitchen with keto friendly foods. Just remember that this list won't tell you everything you need to buy, but it's a good place to get started when trying to figure out a shopping list.

Oils:

- Sesame
- Avocado
- Flaxseed
- Sunflower
- Grape Seed
- Walnut
- Safflower
- Olive
- Coconut
- Canola
- Walnut

Dairy Fats

- Sour Cream
- Cream Cheese
- Cream Fraiche
- Ghee
- Butter (Not Margarine)
- Heavy Creams

Other Fat:

- Pecans
- Olives, Green & Black
- Avocados
- Macadamia Nuts
- Mayonnaise
- Coconut Milk

Protein:

- Lamb
- Pork
- Fresh Eggs
- Chicken
- Beef
- Chicken
- Turkey
- Fish & Shellfish, Frozen & Fresh

Processed Protein:

- Yogurt, Plain
- Whole Milk
- Cheese
- Tofu
- Bacon
- Deli Meats
- Canned Seafood
- Canned Meats

Seeds & Nuts

- Almonds
- Pistachios
- Pumpkin Seeds
- Sesame Seeds
- Chia Seeds
- Flax Meal
- Flax Seeds
- Brazil Nuts

- Pecans
- Almonds
- Almond Flour
- Hazelnuts
- Sunflower Seeds

Vegetables:

- Chicory
- Endive
- Eggplant
- Cucumbers
- Asparagus
- Celery
- Celery Root
- Bell Pepper
- Radish
- Rhubarb
- Swiss Chard
- Spinach
- Onion
- Okra
- Mushrooms
- Kale
- Green Beans
- Carrots
- Bok Choy
- Cauliflower
- Cabbage
- Broccoli
- Lettuce
- Cabbage
- Swiss Chard
- Tomato
- Onion
- Squash
- Brussel Sprouts

Fruit:

- Apricots
- Apples
- Blueberries
- Orange
- Plums
- Raspberries
- Strawberries
- Blackberries
- Cherries
- Guava
- Mango
- Nectarine
- Orange
- Peaches
- Pineapple
- Tangerine
- Watermelon

Sweeteners:

- Stevia
- Swerve
- Splenda
- And Other Non-Sugar Sweeteners

Misc. Items:

- Coconut Flour
- Cocoa Powder, Unsweetened
- Shirataki Noodles
- Yellow Mustard
- Natural Nut Butters, Unsweetened
- Almond Flour

Foods to Avoid

This list includes the foods you should avoid when it comes to the ketogenic diet.

- **All Grains:** Avoid all grains, including whole wheat, quinoa, and white potatoes. This will also include products that are made from grains such as pasta, bread, crackers, cookies, sugar, and sweets.
- **Processed Food:** The ketogenic diet will require you to eat whole foods, so make sure to avoid processed foods when cleaning out your kitchen.
- **Refined Oil or Fat:** While healthy fat is part of the ketogenic diet, it's important to make sure you avoid the unhealthy fat and oil as well.
- **Sweet Drinks & Alcohol:** While alcohol can be fine if it's liquor or unsweetened, you should limit alcohol as much as possible. Sweet drinks such as soda and juice should be avoided too.
- **Tropical Fruit:** There are many fruits to avoid, so make sure that you avoid all tropical fruit unless you look it up. Always check fruit before adding it to your diet.

Your One Week Meal Plan

To properly stay in ketosis and lose the weight you want, you need to limit yourself to twenty net carbs each and every day with no more than a two net carb leeway. It's important to keep as close to the twenty net carbs as possible, and this week long meal plan can help you get started.

Sunday

Breakfast: Tropical Delight

Net Carbs: 4.41 Grams

Lunch: Cheddar & Chive Mug Cake

Net Carbs: 4 Grams

Dinner: Lemon & Thyme Chicken

Net Carbs: 6.5 Grams

Side Dish: Lemon Green Beans

Net Carbs: 6.5 Grams

Snack Allowance: 4.09 Grams

Monday

Breakfast: Keto McMuffin

Net Carbs: 2.9 Grams

Lunch: Easy Pork Salad

Net Carbs: 4.77 Grams

Dinner: Spinach & Scallops

Net Carbs: 7.5 Grams

Snack Allowance: 4.83 Grams

Tuesday

Breakfast: Salmon Breakfast Bombs

Net Carbs: 0.96 Grams

Lunch: Mug Lasagna

Net Carbs: 5.39 Grams

Dinner: Curried Chicken Rolls

Net Carbs: 1.8 Grams

Side Dish: Asian Broccoli Salad

Net Carbs: 3.62 Grams

Snack Allowance: 8.2 Grams

Wednesday

Breakfast: Green Machine Smoothie

Net Carbs: 3 Grams

Lunch: Spinach & Goat Cheese Salad

Net Carbs: 5.8 Grams

Dinner: Pizza Frittata

Net Carbs: 3.9 Grams

Snack Allowance: 7.3 Grams

Thursday

Breakfast: Keto French Toast

Net Carbs: 2.5 Grams

Lunch: Mushroom & Cheese Mug

Net Carbs: 2.4 Grams

Dinner: Fried Fish

Net Carbs: 2.5 Grams

Side Dish: Crispy Kale Sprouts

Net Carbs: 0.82 Grams

Snack Allowance: 11.78

Friday

Breakfast: Cheddar & Chive Omelet

Net Carbs: 1.86

Lunch: Egg & Avocado Salad

Net Carbs: 6.1

Dinner: Pesto Sea Bass

Net Carbs: 1.5 Grams

Side Dish: Sugar Snap Peas with Bacon

Net Carbs: 4.33

Snack Allowance: 6.21

Saturday

Breakfast: Cream Cheese & Salmon Bites

Net Carbs: 0.4 Grams

Lunch: BLT Lettuce Wrap

Net Carbs: 4.1 Grams

Dinner: Zoodle Alfredo

Net Carbs: 7.3 Grams

Snack Allowance: 8.2 Grams

Starting with Breakfast

Breakfast recipes can be the hardest to prepare, especially if you work a busy schedule. Luckily, these recipes are often less than fifteen minutes, so you'll be out the door and ready to start your day in no time at all.

Tropical Delight

Serves: 1

Calories: 355

Fiber: 0 Grams

Fats: 32.63 Grams

Protein: 4.4 Grams

Net Carbs: 4.41 Grams

Ingredients:

- ¼ Cup Sour Cream, Full Fat
- ¾ Cup Coconut Milk, Unsweetened
- 5-7 Ice Cubes
- 1 Tablespoon MCT Oil
- 20 Drops Liquid Stevia
- 2 Tablespoons Flaxseed
- ¼ Teaspoon Banana Extract
- ¼ Teaspoon Blueberry Extract
- ½ Teaspoon Mango Extract

Directions:

1. Blend all ingredients together until completely combined.
2. Serve immediately.

Keto MacMuffin

Serves: 2

Calories: 626

Fiber: 6.5 Grams

Protein: 26.5 Grams

Fat: 54.6 Grams

Net Carbs: 2.9 Grams

Time: 10 Minutes

Ingredients:

Muffins:

- ¼ Cup Almond Flour
- ¼ Teaspoon Baking Soda
- ¼ Cup Flax meal
- 2 Tablespoons Heavy Whipping Cream
- 1 Egg, Large
- ¼ Cup Cheddar Cheese, Grated
- Sea Salt to Taste
- 2 Tablespoon Water

Filling:

- Sea Salt & Pepper to Taste
- 1 Teaspoon Dijon Mustard
- 2 Slices Cheddar Cheese
- 1 Tablespoon Butter
- 2 Eggs, Large
- 1 Tablespoon Ghee

Directions:

1. Place all your dry ingredients for your muffins in a bowl, making sure to mix well.
2. Add in your water, egg and cream, combining with a fork.

3. Grate your cheese adding it to the bowl, and combine well. Place in single serve ramekins for cooking, microwave on high for sixty to ninety seconds.
4. Fry your eggs in ghee, seasoning with salt and pepper. Cook to desired doneness, and then cut your muffins in half. Spread your butter on each half.
5. Top with a cheese slice, egg, and mustard.
6. Enjoy while still warm.

Feta & Spinach Omelet

Serves: 1

Calories: 659

Fiber: 2.8 Grams

Protein: 30.9 Grams

Fat: 55.5 Grams

Net Carbs: 7 Grams

Time: 15 Minutes

Ingredients:

- 3 Eggs, Large
- 1/3 Cup Feta Cheese, Crumbled
- 1 Cup White Mushrooms, Sliced
- 1 Clove Garlic
- 2 Tablespoons Ghee
- 3 Cups Spinach, Fresh
- Sea Salt & Pepper

Directions:

1. Start by preparing your filling. Dice your garlic and place it in a pan with just a tablespoon of your ghee. Season with salt, cooing for a minute over medium-high heat. It should become

fragrant. Add in your mushrooms, stirring and cooking until they're lightly browned. This should take about five minutes.
2. Add in your spinach, cooking for a minute or two until it's wilted.
3. Take off of heat, placing the mixture into a bowl. Drain any excess liquid and then use the pan to cook your omelet.
4. Crack your eggs, mixing with a fork and seasoning with salt and pepper.
5. Pour your eggs into a pan with your ghee, and then coo for thirty seconds. Lower your heat cooking for another minute, and don't try to rush it.
6. When the top of your omelet is almost cooked you will want to add your spinach and mushroom topping, crumbling your feta on top of it. Fold the omelet on half, cooking for another minute and then serve warm.

Chocolate Pancakes

Serves: 2-4

Calories: 215

Fiber: 3.2 Grams

Protein: 11.4 Grams

Fat: 17.3 Grams

Net Carbs: 4.2 Grams

Time: 15 Minutes

Ingredients:

- ½ Teaspoon Baking Soda
- 1 Teaspoon Cream of Tartar
- 1 Teaspoon Cinnamon
- 1/3 Cup + 1 Tablespoon Cacao Powder, Unsweetened
- 4 Eggs, Large
- ½ Cup Ricotta Cheese, Full Fat & Room Temperature

- 2 Tablespoons Ghee
- ¼ Cup Swerve

Directions:

1. Mix all dry ingredients together in a bowl.
2. Crack your eggs in a separate bowl, mixing with your ricotta cheese. Beat until thoroughly combined.
3. Slowly mix in your dry ingredients.
4. Place your ghee in a pan, heating it up and then spoon out small pancakes from the mix. Cook over low-medium for about five minutes. The tops of your pancakes should begin to bubble and therefore firm, and then flip, cooing for another minute to allow your pancake to crisp.
5. Enjoy warm!

Spicy Eggs & Cheese Hash

Serves: 3

Calories: 248

Fiber: 4.03 Grams

Protein: 12.57 Grams

Fat: 18.14 Grams

Net Carbs: 5.77 Grams

Time: 20 Minutes

Ingredients:

- 3 Eggs, Large
- 3 Tablespoons Cotija Cheese
- 2 Teaspoons Tajin Seasoning
- 1 Tablespoon Jalapenos, Sliced
- ½ Avocado, Medium & Sliced
- ¼ Cup Cheddar Cheese, Shredded

- 1 Teaspoon Onion Powder
- 1 Teaspoon Smoked Paprika
- 1 Tablespoon Coconut Oil, Melted
- 5 Ounces Zucchini, Diced
- ½ Red Bell Pepper, Diced
- 6 Ounces Cauliflower, Chopped

Directions:

1. Start by heating your oven to 400.
2. Spread your zucchini, cauliflower, red pepper, and then drizzle with oil. Season with your garlic, paprika and onion powder, making sure to coat well.
3. Cook in a single layer for ten minutes until browned.
4. Remove your vegetables from the oven and top with cheese.
5. Arrange your sliced avocado on another pan, and then crack your eggs in between.
6. Bake for ten minutes, and then top with jalapenos, tajin and cotija cheese.
7. Serve warm.

Salmon Breakfast Bombs

Serves: 2

Calories: 295

Fiber: 0 Grams

Protein: 18.25 Grams

Fat: 23.53 Grams

Net Carbs: 0.96 Grams

Time: 15 Minutes

Ingredients:

- 2 Eggs, Large & Boiled

- Salt & Pepper to Taste
- 2 Tablespoons Chives, Fresh & Chopped
- 4 Ounces Smoked Salmon, Sliced
- ½ Tablespoon Butter, Salted

Hollandaise Sauce:

- 2 Tablespoons Butter, Melted
- 1 Egg Yolk, Large
- ¼ Teaspoon Dijon Mustard
- ½ Tablespoon Water
- 2 Teaspoons Lemon Juice, Fresh
- Salt to Taste

Directions:

1. Heat your pan over high heat, and then add in your butter. Once it's heated, add in your salmon and cook until crisp. Set your salmon aside.
2. Mash your boiled eggs with a fork until fine.
3. Take a pot and add in two cups of water, letting it simmer and then melt your butter for your sauce. Set it to the side, and then whisk your egg yolks, Dijon mustard, salt and lemon juice together. Continue until you see bubbles.
4. Put the bowl over the pot with simmering water to make a double broiler, and whisk until thickened.
5. Pour in your melted butter as it starts to thicken. Stir to avoid clumps. Remove once thickened.
6. Allow it to cool, and then mix in all other ingredients.
7. Make small balls with your hands, and then roll in chives to coat.

Pesto Mug Muffin

Calories: 511

Fiber: 9.4 Grams

Protein: 16.4 Grams

Fat: 46.2 Grams

Net Carbs: 4.5 Grams

Time: 5 Minutes

Ingredients:

- ¼ Cup Flax meal
- 1 Egg, Large
- ¼ Cup Almond Flour
- ¼ Teaspoon Baking Soda
- 2 tablespoon Coconut Milk
- 2 Tablespoons Pesto
- 1 Tablespoon Water

Filling:

- 4 Slices Bacon
- ½ Avocado, Sliced
- 2 Tablespoons Cream Cheese

Directions:

1. Mix all of your ingredients in a bowl, combining well.
2. Add in your milk, egg and water, mixing with a fork.
3. Add in your pesto, dividing between two mugs.
4. Microwave for ninety seconds before serving.

Keto Hash Browns

Serves: 3

Calories: 165

Fiber: 2 Grams

Protein: 7 Grams

Fat: 11.25 Grams

Net Carbs: 3.2 Grams

Time: 20 Minutes

Ingredients:

- ¾ Cup Cheddar Cheese, Shredded
- ¼ Teaspoon Garlic Powder
- ½ Teaspoon Sea Salt
- 1/8 Teaspoon Black Pepper
- ¼ Teaspoon Cayenne Pepper
- 1 Egg, Large
- 3 Cups Cauliflower, Grated

Directions:

1. Microwave your grated cauliflower for three minutes before letting it cool.
2. Place the cauliflower in paper towels, bringing out the excess water that's left.
3. Place the cauliflower in a bowl, combining all of your ingredients.
4. Form six square shapes, and then place on a baking tray that's been greased.
5. Heat your oven to 400, and then bake for fifteen to twenty minutes.
6. Let cool before serving.

Sausage Breakfast

Serves: 4

Calories: 317

Fiber: 1.5 Grams

Protein: 20 Grams

Fat: 23 Grams

Net Carbs: 8 Grams

Time: 20 Minutes

Ingredients:

- 1 Red Bell Pepper, Small & Chunked
- 6 Cremini Mushrooms, Quartered
- ½ Teaspoon Italian Seasoning
- ½ Teaspoon Crushed Red Pepper Flakes
- Salt & Black Pepper to Taste
- 1 Yellow Bell Pepper, Small & Chunked
- 1 Summer Squash, Small & Sliced into Moons
- 1 Zucchini, Small & Sliced into Moons
- 5 Chicken Sausage Links, Sliced
- 2 Cloves Garlic, Minced
- 3 Tablespoons Ghee
- 1 Small Sweet Onion, Chunked

Directions:

1. Melt your ghee over medium heat using a large skillet.
2. Add in your sausage, onion and garlic, cooing for ten minutes.
3. Add in the rest of your ingredients, cooking to your desired doneness. This will take eight to ten minutes. Some people do prefer to cook longer, but it is not necessary.

Green Machine Smoothie

Serves: 1

Calories: 485

Fiber: 20 Grams

Protein: 40 Grams

Fat: 27 Grams

Net Carbs: 3 Grams

Time: 5 Minutes

Ingredients:

- 5 Ice Cubes
- 3 Cups Water
- 2 Cups Spinach, Frozen
- 1 Scoop Whey Protein
- 2 Tablespoons Chia Seeds
- 2 Tablespoons Flax meal
- 1 Tablespoons MCT Oil

Directions:

1. Combine and blend until smooth.

Keto French Toast

Serves: 8

Calories: 437

Fiber: 2 Grams

Protein: 14 Grams

Fat: 42 Grams

Net Carbs: 2.5 Grams

Time: 15 Minutes

Ingredients:

- ¼ Teaspoon Vanilla Extract
- 1 Tablespoon Ghee
- ½ Teaspoon Cinnamon
- 1 Tablespoon Heavy Cream
- 2 Large Slices Bread, Keto Friendly
- 1 Egg, Large

Directions:

1. Cut two slices of bread, cutting each into four sticks.
2. Beat your heavy cream, cinnamon, egg, and vanilla together.

3. Dip the bread sticks into the mixture.
4. Place sticks into a hot skillet, frying on each side before serving warm.

Chocolate & Blackberry Smoothie

Serves: 1

Calories: 346

Fiber: 7.4 Grams

Protein: 2.62 Grams

Fat: 34.17 Grams

Net Carbs: 4.8 Grams

Time: 5 Minutes

Ingredients:

- 7 Ice Cubes
- 2 Tablespoons MCT Oil
- ¼ Teaspoon Xanthan Gum
- 12 Drops Liquid Stevia
- 2 Tablespoons Cocoa Powder, Unsweetened
- ¼ Cup Blackberries, Fresh
- 1 Cup Coconut Milk, Unsweetened

Directions:

1. Blend everything together before serving.

Spinach Scrambled Eggs

Serves: 1

Calories: 713

Fiber: 2.7 Grams

Protein: 41.95 Grams

Fats: 57.23 Grams

Net Carbs: 5.5 Grams

Time: 15 Minutes

Ingredients:

- Sea Salt & Pepper to Taste
- ½ Cup Cheddar Cheese, Shredded
- 4 Cups Spinach, Fresh
- 1 Tablespoon Heavy Cream
- 1 Tablespoon Olive Oil
- 4 Eggs, Large

Directions:

1. Crack your eggs into a bowl, adding in your cream, salt and pepper, mixing well.
2. Add a tablespoon of oil to a pan, heating over high heat.
3. Let the oil reach its smoking point and then add in your spinach, stirring often.
4. Once the spinach has wilted, reduce your heat to medium low and then add in your egg mixture.
5. Mix well, and cook until set. Remember to stir to scramble.
6. Add in your cheese, letting it melt before serving.

Sausage & Feta Omelet

Serves: 1

Calories: 529

Fiber: 0.7 Grams

Protein: 31.38 Grams

Fats: 41.89 Grams

Net Carbs: 5.35 Grams

Time: 15 Minutes

Ingredients:

- 3 Eggs, Large
- Sea Salt & Pepper to Taste
- ½ Tablespoon Olive oil
- ¼ Cup Half & Half
- 1 Tablespoon Feta Cheese
- 1 Cup Spinach, Fresh
- 2 Breakfast Sausages, Cooked & Small

Directions:

1. Heat two pans over medium heat, and split your oil between them.
2. Crack your eggs in a bowl while the oil is heating, scrambling them and stirring in your half and half.
3. Season your egg mixture with salt and pepper.
4. Add your spinach, salt and pepper, sautéing.
5. Cook your sausage in the other pan until browned, and then add to your spinach and set aside.
6. Pour your eggs into the pan that has the drippings from your sausage.
7. Once your egg sets, add your spinach, feta, and sausage in the middle.
8. Flip in half after it's sat for a minute, and cover. Let it cook for two to three minutes more before serving warm.

Cheddar & Chive Omelet

Serves: 1

Calories: 386

Fiber: 0 Grams

Protein: 24.86 Grams

Fat: 30.25 Grams

Net Carbs: 1.86 Grams

Time: 10 Minutes

Ingredients:

- 2 Slices Bacon, Cooked
- Sea Salt & Pepper to Taste
- 1 Ounce Cheddar Cheese, Shredded
- 2 Eggs, Large
- 1 Teaspoon Bacon Fat
- 1 Teaspoon Chives, Fresh & Chopped

Directions:

1. Heat a pan using your bacon fat, keeping it on medium-low heat.
2. Add your eggs, salt, pepper and chives.
3. One your egg sets, add your bacon and cook for thirty seconds.
4. Turn off heat, and then add your cheese on top along with your bacon. Fold your omelet so that it holds the cheese. Leave on heated burner until your cheese is melted.

Banana & Blueberry Bread Smoothie

Serves: 2

Calories: 270

Fiber: 5.65 Grams

Protein: 3.13 Grams

Fat: 23.31 Grams

Net Carb: 4.66 Grams

Time: 5 Minutes

Ingredients:

- 2 Tablespoons MCT Oil
- ¼ Teaspoon Xanthan Gum
- 1 ½ Teaspoon Banana Extract
- 10 Drops Liquid Stevia
- 2 Cups Vanilla Coconut Milk, Unsweetened
- 1 Tablespoon Chia Seeds
- 3 Tablespoons Golden Flaxseed Meal

Directions:

1. Blend everything together until smooth before serving. If you need to thicken add two to three ice cubes to the mix.

Eggs in Purgatory

Serves: 5

Calories: 219

Fiber: 2 Grams

Protein: 9 Grams

Fat: 16 Grams

Net Carbs: 5 Grams

Time: 15 Minutes

Ingredients:

- 5 Breakfast Sausage Links, Precooked & Chopped
- ¼ Cup Onion, Minced
- ½ Cup Zucchini, Diced
- ¼ Teaspoon Pepper
- ¼ Teaspoon Sea Salt, Fine
- 5 Eggs, Large

- 1 Tablespoon Italian Parsley, Chopped
- 1 Tablespoon Parmesan, Grated
- 2 Leaves Basil, Torn
- 1 Tablespoon Olive Oil
- 1/8 Teaspoon Oregano, Dried
- 1/3 Cup Red Bell Pepper, Diced
- 2 Cloves Garlic, Minced
- 1 ½ Cups Tomato Puree

Directions:

1. Heat your olive oil in a skillet using medium heat, and then add in your bell peppers, garlic, onion and stir. Cook for about five minutes. Your onions should become translucent.
2. Add your chopped sausage and zucchini, cooking for another four minutes. Your zucchini should begin to soften.
3. Add in your basil, oregano, salt, pepper and tomato sauce, stirring to combine and cooking for three to five minutes. The sauce should bubble and start to reduce a little.
4. Make a depression with a spoon in the sauce, and then crack in egg into each one.
5. Cover your pan, and turn the heat down to load. Allow to simmer for eight to twelve minutes or until your eggs reach the desired doneness.
6. Top with parmesan and parsley before serving.

Cream Cheese & Salmon Bites

Serves: 12

Calories: 32

Fiber: 0 Grams

Protein: 1.9 Grams

Fat: 2.2 Grams

Net Carbs: 0.4 Grams

Time: 20 Minutes

Ingredients:

- ½ Ounce Cream Cheese, Full Fat
- 2 eggs
- ¼ Teaspoon Sea Salt
- ½ Ounce Cheddar Cheese, Grated
- ½ Teaspoon Dill, Dried
- ½ Ounce Smoked Salmon, Sliced
- 5 ½ Tablespoons Cream

Directions:

1. Whisk your eggs, milk and salt into a jug.
2. Fold in your cheese, smoked salmon, cream cheese and dill.
3. Pour into mini muffins, baking at 350 for ten to fifteen minutes.

Lunch Recipes

Lunch can be difficult when you're on a diet, but these ketogenic diet recipes are easy to cook in under twenty minutes. The best part of these lunch recipes is most of them can be packed up and taken with you so that you can ignore temptations and stick to the diet you're working on. Remember that if you want the ketogenic diet to work, you have to keep your body in ketosis. This means that you can't have cheat days, so a portable lunch is often vital to your success.

Easy Pork Salad

Serves: 2

Calories: 537.5

Fiber: 1.85 Grams

Protein: 12.74 Grams

Fat: 51.46 Grams

Net Carbs: 4.77 Grams

Time: 15 Minutes

Ingredients:

- 4.58 Ounces Pork Belly Slices, Cooked
- 1 Teaspoon Water
- 20 Grams Walnut Halves
- 2 Teaspoons Sea Salt
- ½ Teaspoon Wholegrain Mustard
- 2 Teaspoons Olive Oil
- 2.12 Ounces Mixed Green
- 2 Tablespoons White Wine Vinegar
- ¼ Pear, Medium
- 1.5 Ounces Blue Cheese
- 1 Tablespoons Stevia

Directions:

1. Chop your walnut halves into even smaller pieces, and then heat a pan over medium-high heat.
2. Add your stevia and water to the pan, dissolving your stevia, and then add your walnuts. Cook for about five minutes. Your nuts should caramelize and the liquid should start to thicken.
3. Crumble your cheese and your chop your pear.
4. Mix your mustards, white wine, and olive oil in a bowl to make your vinaigrette.
5. Toss all ingredients together before serving.

Mug Melt

Serves: 1

Calories: 268

Fiber: 0 Grams

Protein: 22.4 Grams

Fat: 17.99 Grams

Net Carbs: 3.83 Grams

Time: 5 Minutes

Ingredients:

- 2 Ounces Roast Beef (Deli Slices)
- 1 ½ Ounces Pepper Jack Cheese, Shredded
- 1 Tablespoon Sour Cream, Full Fat
- 1 ½ Tablespoons Green Chiles, Diced
- Smoked Paprika to Taste

Directions:

1. Place half your roast beef at the bottom of your mug. You may want to break it into small pieces first.

2. Spread a half a tablespoon of sour cream over it, and then top with a half a tablespoon of green chile.
3. Layer in a half an hour of cheese, and then repeat the layering.
4. Finish off with the last of your cheese and then top with paprika.
5. Cook for one to two minutes in the microwave.

Mug Lasagna

Serves: 1

Calories: 318

Fiber: 1.1 Grams

Protein: 20.45 Grams

Fat: 23.54 Grams

Net Carbs: 5.39 Grams

Time: 5 Minutes

Ingredients:

- 3 Ounces Mozzarella Cheese, Whole Mil
- 2 Tablespoons Ricotta Cheese, Whole Milk
- 1/3 Zucchini, Medium & Sliced
- 3 Tablespoons Marinara Sauce

Directions:

1. Place some marinara at the bottom of your dish, and then layer some zucchini on top.
2. Spread out a tablespoon of ricotta and then another tablespoon of marinara.
3. Continue layering like this and then top with mozzarella.
4. Microwave for three to four minutes.

Simple Mixed Green Salad

Serves: 1

Calories: 393

Fiber: 1.83 Grams

Protein: 13.87 Grams

Fat: 36.11 Grams

Net Carbs: 4.27 Grams

Time: 10 Minutes

Ingredients:

- 2 Slices Bacon
- Sea Salt & Pepper to Taste
- 3 Tablespoons Pine Nuts, Roasted
- 2 Ounces Mixed Greens
- 2 Tablespoons Parmesan
- 2 Tablespoons Keto Vinaigrette

Directions:

1. Start by cooking your bacon until it's crisp, and then crumble once cooled.
2. Add all ingredients together before serving.

Easy Keto Soup

Serves: 6

Calories: 392

Fiber: 2.9 Grams

Protein: 4.9 Grams

Fat: 37.6 Grams

Net Carbs: 6.8 Grams

Time: 20 Minutes

Ingredients:

- 1 Cauliflower, Medium
- 1 Teaspoon Sea Salt
- ¼ Cup Ghee
- 1 Cup Cream
- 4 Cups Vegetable Stock
- 7.1 Ounces Spinach, Fresh
- 5.3 Ounces Watercress
- 1 Bay Leaf, Crumbled
- 1 White Onion, Medium
- 2 Cloves Garlic, Minced
- Black Pepper to Taste

Directions:

1. Dice your onion, and then cook over medium high heat until browned, adding in your garlic.
2. Cut your cauliflower into small pieces, and add to the onion.
3. Crumble your bay leaf, and then cook for another five minutes. You'll need to stir frequently.
4. Add the watercress and spinach, cooing for two to three more minutes.
5. Add in your vegetable stock, bringing it to a boil and cook until your cauliflower is tender but crisp.
6. Add in your cream, seasoning with salt and pepper.
7. Use an immersion blender and blend until completely smooth.
8. Serve immediately.

Easy Tuna Salad

Serves: 1

Calories: 626

Fiber: 1.5 Grams

Protein: 41.4 Grams

Fat: 49.7 Grams

Net Carbs: 3.9 Grams

Time: 5 Minutes

Ingredients:

- 1 Head Lettuce, Small
- 5 Ounces Tuna, Drained
- 2 Eggs, Hard Boiled
- 1 Tablespoon Lemon Juice, Fresh
- 2 Tablespoons Mayonnaise
- 1 Tablespoon Olive Oil
- 1 Spring Onion, Medium
- Sea Salt to Taste

Directions:

1. Tear your lettuce, and then wash and dry.
2. Place in a serving bowl. Add in your tuna once it's drained.
3. Top with your boiled eggs.
4. Mix together your lemon juice and mayonnaise. Drizzle over the tuna, and then top with spring onions.
5. Drizzle your olive oil over the top before serving.

Egg & Avocado Salad

Serves: 2

Calories: 436

Fiber: 7.6 Grams

Protein: 17 Grams

Fat: 36.3 Grams

Net Carbs: 6.1 Grams

Time: 15 Minutes

Ingredients:

- 1 Avocado, Large
- 4 Eggs, Large
- 4 Cups Mixed Lettuce
- Sea Salt & Pepper to Taste
- 2 Teaspoons Dijon Mustard
- 2 Cloves Garlic, Crushed
- ½ Cup Sour Cream, Full Fat

Directions:

1. Boil your eggs as you normally would, and then let cool and peel.
2. Mix your sour cream, Dijon mustard, salt, pepper and garlic together to make your dressing.
3. Add your greens to a salad bowl, slicing your avocado and putting it on top.
4. Quarter your eggs and add them in, and then season with salt and pepper. Add dressing and enjoy.

Mackerel Salad

Serves: 2

Calories: 133

Fiber: 8.5 Grams

Protein: 27.3 Grams

Fat: 49.9 Grams

Net Carbs: 7.6 Grams

Time: 20 Minutes

Ingredients:

- 2 Eggs, Large
- 2 Mackerel Fillets
- 4 Cups Mixed Lettuce
- 2 Cups Green Beans
- 1 Avocado, Medium
- 1 Tablespoon Ghee
- ¼ Teaspoon Sea Salt
- Pepper to Taste

Mustard & Lemon Dressing:

- 2 Tablespoons Olive Oil
- 2 Tablespoons Lemon Juice, Fresh
- 1 Teaspoon Dijon Mustard

Directions:

1. Boil your eggs in a large pot of salted water, which will take about ten minutes.
2. Let cool before peeling.
3. Cook your green beans in a saucepan of water, adding salt.
4. Once they're at a boil, cook for four to five minutes, allowing them to become tender and crisp.
5. Remove from heat and drain your water.
6. Lightly score your mackerel fillets, and then season with salt and pepper.
7. Heat ghee in a large pan, and then add in your fillets. Make sure you place the skin down, and then cook until the meat is fully cooked. The skin should become crisp.
8. Mix all dressing ingredients together.
9. Wash and drain your lettuce, and then place in a bowl. Top with your green beans.
10. Quarter your eggs, and place on top of your green beans. Add your mackerel fillets, and drizzle with your dressing before serving.

Chive & Cheddar Mug Cake

Serves: 1

Calories: 546

Fiber: 2.3 Grams

Protein: 20.1 Grams

Fat: 49.95 Grams

Net Carbs: 4 Grams

Time: 5 Minutes

Ingredients:

- 1 Egg, Large
- ½ Teaspoon Baking Powder
- 2 Tablespoons Almond Flour
- 2 Tablespoons Butter
- 1 Tablespoon White Cheddar, Shredded
- 1 Tablespoon Chives, Fresh & Chopped
- Sea Salt & Pepper to Taste
- 1 Tablespoon Sharp Cheddar, Shredded
- 1 Tablespoon Almond Flour
- 2 Slices Bacon, Cooked & Chopped

Directions:

1. Add your egg and two tablespoons of butter into a cup.
2. Mix well, and then add in your bacon, flour, chives, and cheese, mixing well.
3. Microwave on high for sixty-five seconds.

Egg Drop Soup

Serves: 1

Calories: 289

Fiber: 0 Grams

Protein: 15.3 Grams

Fat: 23.24 Grams

Net Carbs: 2.92 Grams

Time: 5 Minutes

Ingredients:

- 2 Eggs, Large
- 1 Teaspoon Chili Garlic Paste
- ½ Cup Chicken Bouillon
- 1 ½ Cups Chicken Broth
- 1 Tablespoon Bacon Fat

Directions:

1. Put a pan over medium-high heat. Add in your chicken broth, bacon fat and bouillon cube. Bring it to a boil, stirring everything together.
2. Add in your chili paste, and then turn your stove off.
3. Beat your eggs together, and then pour into the broth while it's still steaming.
4. Stir together, and let it sit so that the egg cooks for a moment.

Jalapeno Mug Cake

Serves: 1

Calories: 455

Fiber: 3.7 Grams

Protein: 15.38 Grams

Fat: 41.15 Grams

Net Carbs: 4.43 Grams

Time: 5 Minutes

Ingredients:

- ½ Teaspoon Baking Powder
- ¼ Teaspoon Sea Salt, Fine
- 1 Slice Bacon, Cooked
- 1 Tablespoon Cream Cheese, Full Fat
- 1 Egg, Large
- ½ Jalapeno Pepper, Medium
- 1 Tablespoon Butter
- 2 Tablespoons Almond Flour
- 1 Tablespoon Golden Flaxseed Meal

Directions:

1. Start by crumbling your cooked bacon.
2. Slice your jalapenos, removing the seeds.
3. Mix all ingredients together in a mug, and microwave on high for seventy-five seconds.

Spinach & Goat Cheese Salad

Serves: 2

Calories: 645

Fiber: 4 Grams

Protein: 33.2 Grams

Fat: 54.2 Grams

Net Carbs: 5.8 Grams

Time: 20 Minutes

Ingredients:

- ½ Cup Goat Cheese, Hard & Grated
- ½ Cup Flaked Almonds, Toasted

- 4 Tablespoons Keto Vinaigrette
- 4 Cups Spinach, Fresh

Directions:

1. Turn your oven to 400, and then line a baking tray with parchment paper that's been cut in half. Grate your cheese on the baking sheet, splitting it between both halves.
2. Form into small circles, and then bake for ten minutes. The cheese should be golden, but it shouldn't brown yet.
3. Remove from the oven, and then let it cool.
4. Set a bowl upside down, and then flip your cheese over it. Let it cool in this position for five minutes.
5. Wash your spinach and then pat dry, and then place it into your cheese bowls. Add all of your other ingredients, and toss to combine before serving.

Bacon & Avocado Salad

Serves: 2

Calories: 699

Fiber: 15.5 Grams

Protein: 14.2 Grams

Fat: 65.6 Grams

Net Carbs: 6.7 Grams

Time: 20 Minutes

Ingredients:

- 2 Heads Lettuce, Small
- 2 Avocados, Large
- 1 Spring Onion, Medium
- 4 Slices Bacon, Large
- 2 Cups Spinach, Fresh

- 2 Eggs, Hard Boiled & Slices

Vinaigrette:

- 1 Tablespoon Apple Cider Vinegar
- 3 Tablespoons Olive Oil
- 1 Teaspoon Dijon Mustard
- Sea Salt & Pepper to Taste

Directions:

1. Start by cooking your bacon to a crisp, and then add a ½ cup of water to render the fat. This will take ten to fifteen minutes. Set it to the side.
2. Tear your lettuce and wash, and then wash your spinach. Dry your greens, and then halve your avocados. Slice them into strips, and mix all ingredients to make your vinaigrette.
3. Peel your eggs and then slice them.
4. Crumble your bacon, and then add all ingredients together and enjoy.

Mushroom & Cheese Mug

Serves: 2

Calories: 434

Fiber: 6.5 Grams

Protein: 18.7 Grams

Fat: 37.2 Grams

Net Carbs: 2.4 Grams

Time: 15 Minutes

Ingredients:

- ¼ Cup Flax meal
- ¼ Cup Almond Flour

- ¼ Teaspoon Baking Soda
- 2 Tablespoons Water
- 2 Tablespoons Cream
- 1 Egg, Large
- 1 Tablespoon Ghee
- Sea Salt to Taste

Filling:

1. ¼ Cup Mushrooms, Sliced
2. ½ Cup Cheddar Cheese, Diced
3. 1 Tablespoon Basil, Chopped
4. 2 Slices Bacon, Crumbled & Cooked

Directions:

1. Cook your mushrooms in your ghee until browned. This should take three to five minutes.
2. Place all dry ingredients in a bowl, mixing well.
3. Add in your water, cream and egg, mixing well.
4. Add your bacon and mushrooms, mixing well.
5. Divide between two mugs, and then add in your cheddar and basil.
6. Cook for sixty to ninety seconds each.
7. Let sit before serving.

BLT Lettuce Wrap

Serves: 1

Calories: 244

Fiber: 3.4 Grams

Protein: 11.9 Grams

Fat: 19.6 Grams

Net Carbs: 4.1 Grams

Time: 5 Minutes

Ingredients:

- 3-4 Lettuce Leaves
- 2 Slices Bacon, Cooked
- 3 Slices Tomato
- ¼ Avocado, Small & Sliced

Ranch Dressing:

- Sea Salt & Pepper to Taste
- ¼ Teaspoon Onion Powder
- 1 Tablespoon Mayonnaise
- 1 Teaspoon Lemon Juice, Fresh
- ¼ Teaspoon Garlic Powder
- 1 Teaspoon Parsley, Dried

Directions:

1. Mix all of your ranch ingredients together.
2. Place a piece of parchment on your counter, and then place your lettuce on top in a layer with the leaves slightly overlapping. Drizzle with ranch.
3. Top with your bacon and tomato.
4. Add your avocado and roll like a wrap.
5. Cut in half before serving.

Dinner Recipes

Dinner is an important meal of a day which can be difficult if you don't have a lot of time to spare. So many dinner recipes take forever to cook, so here are some main dishes you can cook in twenty minutes or less. Remember that when you're on the keto diet, you don't need a side dish. Eat what you want, when you want to, as long as you stay within twenty net carbs a day so that you can stay in ketosis.

Zoodle Alfredo

Serves: 8

Calories: 742

Fiber: 1.6 Grams

Protein: 15.5 Grams

Fat: 73.2 Grams

Net Carbs: 7.3 Grams

Ingredients:

- 2 ½ lbs Zucchini, Spiralized
- 4 Tablespoons Olive Oil

Sauce:

- 2 Cloves Garlic, Minced
- ¾ Cup Butter, Unsalted
- 6 Ounces Cream Cheese
- 6 Ounces Parmesan Cheese
- ¾ Cup Cheddar Cheese, Grated
- 1 ½ Pints Heavy Cream
- 1 Tablespoon Basil, Chopped
- 1 Teaspoon Oregano, Chopped
- Sea Salt & Pepper to Taste

Directions:

1. Start by sprializing your noodles.
2. Place in a colander, and then sprinkle with salt. Place it in your sink so that it can drain.
3. Melt your butter in a pan, and then add in the garlic.
4. Add in your cream, bringing it to a simmer.
5. Add your cream cheese, and add in a quarter of your shredded cheeses. You'll want to stir to make sure that the cheese melts.
6. Add your cheese in batches, and don't worry about how slow it melts. Just turn up the heat and continue to stir.
7. Mix in your herbs once all of your cheese is melted.
8. Take off of the heat, letting it sit and thicken.
9. Pat your zoodles dry, and then pour your oil into a pan. Toss the zoodles in, sautéing them quickly for about one to two minutes. They should soften. Make sure you do not overcook them.
10. Place in a serving dish, and top with Alfredo. Finish with some grated cheese. Serve warm.

Thai Inspired Pork Salad

Serves: 2

Calories: 721

Fiber: 5.2 Grams

Protein: 41 Grams

Fat: 55.3 Grams

Net Carbs: 9.3 Grams

Time: 20 Minutes

Ingredients:

- 1 Tablespoon Coconut Oil
- 4 Green Onions, Sliced Thin
- 3 Cloves Garlic, Minced

- 2" Ginger, Minced
- 1 lb Ground Pork, 20% Fat
- Handful Mixed Herbs (Mint, Cilantro & Thai Basil)
- 1 Tablespoon Fish Sauce
- 1 Teaspoon Zest
- 1 Tablespoon Coconut Aminos
- 2 Shallots, Small & Sliced Thin
- ½ Teaspoon White Pepper
- 1 Teaspoon Red Pepper Flakes
- 3 Tablespoons Lime Juice, Fresh
- 1 Bag Kelp Noodles (12 Ounces)
- Lettuce Cups for Serving

Directions:

1. Heat your coconut oil in a skillet and add in your shallot and pork, cooking for six to eight minutes. Break your pork into small pieces using a wooden spoon, and once it's browned.
2. Place your coconut aminos, lime juice and zest, red pepper flakes, white pepper, fish sauce, and green onions together as well as half of your herbs.
3. Add your herb mixture into the can, and then cook for a minute.
4. Add your sauce, and then stir well.
5. Take off of heat and add in your remaining herbs. Add in your salt and then place in lettuce cups to serve. Top with kelp noodles.

Fried Fish

Serves: 4

Calories: 464

Fiber: 4.4 Grams

Protein: 35 Grams

Fat: 33.5 Grams

Net Carbs: 2.5 Grams

Time: 20 Minutes

Ingredients:

- 4 Fillets Cod (1.3lbs)
- Pinch Caraway Seeds, Ground
- Sea Salt & Pepper to Taste
- ¼ Cup Ghee
- 4 Tablespoons Flax meal
- 1 Cup Almond Flour
- 1 Egg, Large
- 1 Tablespoon Heavy Whipping Cream

Directions:

1. In a bowl mix your flax meal and almond flour, and then pat your fish dry.
2. Season with salt, pepper and caraway on both sides of your fish.
3. Crack your egg in a bowl, beating it before adding cream and a pinch of salt.
4. Dip your fish in it, and then dip it in the almond and flax mixture.
5. Shake off any excess coating, and then set it to the side.
6. Add your ghee to a pan, heating it up and then add in your fish.
7. Fry for two to three minutes on each side. Make sure that your pan is hot before you add the fish, and turning them too soon will cause the breading to fall off.
8. Serve warm.

Pesto Sea Bass

Serves: 2

Calories: 423

Fiber: 0.7 Grams

Protein: 29.3 Grams

Fat: 32.9 Grams

Net Carbs: 1.5 Grams

Time: 15 Minutes

Ingredients:

- 1 Tablespoon Ghee
- 2 Large Fillets Sea Bass, 10.6 Ounces
- 1 Tablespoon Lemon Juice, Fresh
- 4 Tablespoons Pesto
- Sea Salt to Taste

Directions:

1. Heat your oven to 400, and then line a baking sheet with baking paper. Put your sea bass on the baking sheet with your skin side down.
2. Season with salt and pepper and then brush down with ghee. Squeeze your lemon over it, and then cook for ten minutes.
3. Remove from the oven, and then put two tablespoons of pesto over each, brushing it over smoothly.
4. Place back in the oven and cook for another three to five minutes.
5. Remove it from the oven, letting it cool before serving.

Keto Pizza

Serves: 4

Calories: 510

Fiber: 2.6 Grams

Protein: 29.6 Grams

Fat: 41.4 Grams

Net Carbs: 5.7 Grams

Time: 20 Minutes

Ingredients:

- 1 ½ Cups Mozzarella Cheese, Grated
- 1 Egg, Large
- ½ Teaspoon Sea Salt, Fine
- 2 Tablespoons Cream Cheese
- ¾ Cup + 1 Tablespoon Almond Flour
- Olive Oil

Topping:

- 2 Jalapeno Peppers, Sliced
- 3 Ounces Pepperoni
- ¼ Cup Marinara Sauce, Sugar Free
- ½ Cup Mozzarella Cheese, Grated
- 1/3 Cup Parmesan Cheese, Grated
- 3 Ounces Pepperoni
- Basil, Fresh

Directions:

1. Place your mozzarella cheese in a bowl with your cream cheese, microwaving for a minute. Mix and then microwave again for a half a minute more.
2. Add in your egg, mixing well and then add in your almond flour and salt. Continue to mix until combined.
3. Use your oil on your hands so the dough doesn't stick, and then flatten the dough on a heatproof baking mat. Make sure to flatten it to about ¼ inch thick.
4. Bake for twelve to fifteen minutes at 425.
5. Spread marinara on top, and then add your toppings. Bake for another two to five minutes.

Pizza Frittata

Serves: 2-4

Calories: 426

Fiber: 1 Gram

Protein: 25.4 Grams

Fat: 33.4 Grams

Net Carbs: 3.9 Grams

Ingredients:

- 6 Eggs, Large
- 1/3 Cup Marinara Sauce, Sugar Free
- 3 Ounces Pepperoni, chopped
- 1 Small Onion, Diced
- 1 Red Bell Pepper, Sliced
- 1 Tablespoon Ghee
- 1/3 Cup Mozzarella Cheese, Grated
- 1/3 Cup Parmesan Cheese, Grated
- ½ Teaspoon Oregano, Dried

Topping:

- 1 Ounce Pepperoni Slices
- ¼ Cup Mozzarella Cheese, Grated
- ¼ Cup Parmesan Cheese, Grated
- Basil for Garnish

Directions:

1. Crack your eggs and beat in a bowl, adding in your oregano, grated parmesan, grated mozzarella and your marinara together.
2. Grease your pan with your ghee, and then add in your pepperoni. Cook over medium-high heat until it is crisp.
3. Add in your onion, cooking for a few more minutes.
4. Add your red bell pepper and then cook until tender and crisp.

5. Pour the egg mixture on top, and then let it firm around the edges. This will take eight to ten minutes.
6. Top with your remaining cheese as well as your pepperoni slices, letting it broil for five to six minutes.
7. Remove from your oven, and then top with basil before serving.

Spicy Prawn Rolls

Serves: 4

Calories: 464

Fiber: 6.3 Grams

Protein: 19.2 Grams

Fat: 39.4 Grams

Net Carbs: 5.8 Grams

Time: 20 Minutes

Ingredients:

- 10.6 Ounces Prawn or Shrimp, Cooked
- 1 Tablespoon Sriracha Chili Sauce
- ¼ Cup Mayonnaise

Hand Rolls:

- 1 Tablespoon Rice Vinegar
- 1 Avocado, Large & Sliced
- ½ Teaspoon Sea Salt
- ¼ Cup Mayonnaise
- 2 Tablespoons Ghee
- 1 Cauliflower, Medium
- 4 Nori Seaweed Sheets

Directions:

1. Place your prawns into a bowl and then add your sriracha sauce, mayonnaise, and then season with salt. Make sure to mix well.
2. Prepare your cauli-rice by cutting your cauliflower into florets, and then process in a food processor. Cook in a hot pan that's greased with your ghee for seven to eight minutes. You should do this using medium heat, and then season with salt, making sure to stir often.
3. Place in a bowl, letting it cool.
4. Add in your mayonnaise and vinegar, combining well. This should be sticky.
5. Top your nori sheets with the rice and then the spicy prawns. Add your avocado on top, and then roll tightly into a cone shape.

Curried Chicken Rolls

Serves: 4

Calories: 265

Fiber: 1.1 Grams

Protein: 23 Grams

Fat: 17.8 Grams

Net Carbs: 1.8 Grams

Time: 10 Minutes

Ingredients:

- 1/3 Cup Sour Cream, Full Fat
- ¼ Teaspoon Turmeric Powder
- ½ Teaspoon Curry Powder
- ½ Teaspoon Sea Salt
- ½ Teaspoon Chili Powder
- 2 Cloves Garlic, Minced
- 2 Teaspoons Grated Ginger, Fresh

Rolls:

- 2 Tablespoons Ghee
- 4 Eggs, Large
- 1 ½ Cups Chicken, Cooked & Shredded
- ¼ Cup Chives, Chopped & Fresh
- 4 Nori Seaweed Sheets

Directions:

1. Mix all of your dressing ingredients together, making sure it's combined.
2. Place your chicken in a bowl, adding your dressing over it. Add in your chopped chives, combining with a fork before setting it to the side.
3. Prepare your omelets by cracking an egg into a bowl and seasoning with salt one at a time.
4. Whisk and pour into the hot pan that's been greased with ghee. Repeat for the remaining three eggs, cooking to desired doneness.
5. Assemble your roles with an omelet on top of your nori sheet, adding your curried chicken on top of that.
6. Roll into a cone shape before serving.

Lemon & Thyme Chicken

Serves: 4

Calories: 677

Fiber: 0.1 Grams

Protein: 28.2 Grams

Fat: 61.3 Grams

Net Carbs: 1 Gram

Time: 20 Minutes

Ingredients:

- 1 Tablespoon Thyme, Fresh & Chopped
- 2 Tablespoons Lemon Juice, Fresh
- 1 Teaspoon Lemon Zest
- 2 Cloves Garlic, Minced
- 2 Tablespoon Ghee
- 1 Teaspoon Sea Salt
- 2 Tablespoon Olive Oil
- ¼ Teaspoon Black Pepper
- 8 Chicken Thighs, Deboned

Directions:

1. Prepare your chicken thighs by cutting the bone out. Trim any excess fat.
2. Place the thighs with the skin side down on a cutting board, flattening with a meat pounder.
3. Layer the thighs in a bowl, seasoning with your garlic, salt, pepper, olive oil, thyme, lemon juice and lemon zest.
4. For a better flavor you can choose to refrigerate for an hour. Pat dry of marinade. Pat the skin side off with a paper towel.
5. Heat your ghee in a pan over medium-high, and then place your thighs in skin side down.
6. Cook for seven to ten minutes, and then flip over. Cook for another two to three minutes before serving.

Bunless BBQ Burgers

Serves: 4

Fiber: 9.5 Grams

Protein: 25.4 Grams

Fat: 40.7 Grams

Net Carbs: 8 Grams

Time: 20 Minutes

Ingredients:

- 1 Tablespoon Thyme, Fresh & Chopped
- 1 Tablespoon Dijon Mustard
- 1 Tablespoon Oregano, Fresh & Chopped
- 1.1 lbs Minced Beef
- Sea Salt & Pepper to Taste
- 2 Cloves Garlic, Crushed
- 14.1 Ounces Iceberg Lettuce

Directions:

1. Cover your avocado with foil to keep your avocado from browning, and then place your beef into a bowl. Add your thyme, oregano, garlic, salt, pepper and mustard into the meat, mixing well.
2. Divide into four parts to make four larger burgers.
3. Cook immediately to desired doneness in a pan with light oil or grill them for eight to ten minutes. You should flip your burgers halfway through to make sure they get completely done through the middle.
4. Fold your lettuce leaves into a serving bowl and top with your burgers. Some people prefer to top with guacamole as well.

Meatballs on a Stick

Serves: 4 (8 Skewers)

Calories: 641

Fiber: 1.1 Gram

Protein: 40 Grams

Fat: 50.6 Grams

Net Carbs: 2.9 Grams

Time: 20 Minutes

Ingredients:

- 1.3 lbs Ground Beef
- 1 Egg, Large
- 1 Tablespoon Paprika
- 1 Teaspoon Lemon Zest, Fresh
- ½ Teaspoon Sea Salt, Fine
- 7.1 Ounces Spanish Chorizo
- 2 Cloves Garlic, Crushed
- ½ Red Onion, Medium
- 1 Tablespoon Oregano, Fresh
- 2 Tablespoons Basil, Fresh

Directions:

1. Dice your onion, and then place your meat in a mixing bowl.
2. Add your garlic, lemon zest, chopped herbs, onion, egg and paprika into the bowl, combining with your hands.
3. Slice your chorizo sausage, and then make 24 meatballs with your beef mixture.
4. Layer your skewers with a meatball between two sausage slices.
5. Barbeque for seven to eight minutes on high. It should be fully cooked and crispy on the outside.

Spinach & Scallops

Serves: 5

Calories: 469

Fiber: 5.5 Grams

Protein: 30.3 Grams

Fat: 33.7 Grams

Net Carbs: 7.5 Grams

Time: 20 Minutes

Ingredients:

- 1 lb Scallops, Raw
- 2 Tablespoons Ghee
- 2 lbs Spinach
- ½ Spanish Chorizo Sausage (4.2 Ounces)
- 2 Cloves Garlic
- ½ Teaspoon Sea Salt
- 2 Tablespoons Lemon Juice, Fresh
- Pepper to Taste
- 1 Cup Parmesan Cheese, Grated Fine
- ¼ Cup Heavy Whipping Cream

Directions:

1. Dice your sausage, and then place your sausage in a greased pan once it's hot. Cook with a tablespoon of ghee over medium-high heat until crisp. This should take three to five minutes.
2. Use a slotted spoon so you don't get too much grease with your sausage and place it in a bowl once cooked.
3. Wash your scallops under cold water and prepare them. The roe, also known as coral, and the white muscle are the only edible parts of your scallop.
4. Clean your scallops under cold water again once prepared, and then halve them widthwise, removing the scallop from the roe. Season with salt.
5. Use the pan that you cooked your sausage in and place your scallops in them once it's hot. Make sure they're in a single layer, and hen cook on one side for two minutes before flipping them over and repeating. If you find your scallop to be stuck just wait another few seconds before flipping. Each side should be lightly golden, and they should be opaque when fully cooked. If you overcook your scallops they'll become chewy and tough.
6. Repeat with the remaining scallops as well as the roe. Return them to the pan once cooked adding in your sausage, cooking for thirty to sixty seconds. When done, peel your garlic and dice it. Add to the pan with your remaining ghee. Cook until fragrant, and stir.

7. Add your spinach, stirring well and then pour in your cream. Cook for another minute, topping with grated parmesan and taking it from heat. Set it to the side.
8. Place your creamed spinach on a plate, topping with scallops and sausage. Drizzle with your fresh lemon juice and garnish with pepper and parsley before serving.

Perfect Pork Chops

Serves: 6

Calories: 399

Fiber: 0.85 Grams

Protein: 29.4 Grams

Fat: 28.1 Grams

Net Carbs: 4.7 Grams

Time: 15 Minutes

Ingredients:

- 2 Tablespoons Ghee
- Sea Salt & Pepper
- 6 Pork Chops, Medium (1.76 lbs)

Directions:

1. Pat your pork chops dry with a paper towel, and then rub down with a tablespoon of ghee on both sides. Season your pork chops using your salt and pepper.
2. Use your remaining ghee to grease a pan, and get the pan hot before adding your pork chops. Turn the heat to medium-high, and cook until the sides start to brown, which will take about two minutes on each side.
3. Lower your heat and cook for another five to ten minutes.
4. Let rest for five minutes before serving.

Stuffed Avocado with Cajun Chicken

Serves: 2

Calories: 638

Fiber: 11 Grams

Protein: 34.5 Grams

Fat: 50.6 Grams

Net Carbs: 5.4 Grams

Time: 5 Minutes

Ingredients:

- 1 Teaspoon Thyme, Dried
- 1 Teaspoon Paprika
- ¼ Teaspoon Cayenne Pepper
- 2 Tablespoon Lemon Juice, Fresh
- 2 Avocados, Medium & Seeded
- 1 ½ Cup Chicken, Cooked
- ¼ Cup Mayonnaise
- 2 Tablespoon Sour Cream
- ½ Teaspoon Onion Powder
- ¼ Teaspoon Cayenne Pepper
- ½ Teaspoon Garlic Powder

Directions:

1. Shred your chicken into small pieces, and then add your thyme, onion powder, paprika, sour cream, mayonnaise, garlic, and cayenne pepper.
2. Next add in your lemon juice and season to taste with your salt, mixing well.
3. Scoop the middle of each avocado out, leaving it with a half an inch to an inch of flesh, and then fill your avocado with the mixture.

4. Serve and enjoy.

Cheesy "Risotto"

Serves: 4

Calories: 366

Fiber: 4 Grams

Protein: 17.4 Grams

Fat: 28.8 Grams

Net Carbs: 7.6 Grams

Time: 20 Minutes

Ingredients:

- 6 Cups Cauli-Rice
- ¼ Cup Ghee
- 1 Cup Chicken Stock
- 1 White Onion, Small & Chopped Fine
- 1 Teaspoon Dijon Mustard
- 1 Cup Cheddar Cheese, Shredded
- 1 Cup Parmesan Cheese, Grated
- 2-4 Tablespoons Chives, Chopped Fresh
- Sea Salt to Taste

Directions:

1. Start by greasing a pan with your ghee, and then add your chopped onion once hot. Cook over medium heat, browning it slightly. Add in your cauli-rice, mixing well.
2. Cook for a few minutes but be careful not to overcook, and then add in your chicken stock. Cook for five minutes. Your rice should become both tender and crisp.
3. Grate your cheddar and parmesan, and then add in mustard to your pan, taking it off of heat.

4. Add in your cheese, mixing well. Keep a little parmesan to garnish, and then add in your chopped chives. Season with salt and pepper.
5. Top with remaining parmesan and enjoy while still warm.

Egg Stuffed Avocado

Serves: 2

Calories: 616

Fiber: 10.6 Grams

Protein: 16.5 Grams

Fat: 56.8 Grams

Net Carbs: 4.8 Grams

Time: 15 Minutes

Ingredients:

- 2 Avocados, Medium & Seeded
- 4 Eggs, Large
- 2 Spring Onions, Medium
- Sea Salt & Pepper to Taste
- 1 Teaspoon Dijon Mustard
- 2 Tablespoons Sour Cream
- ¼ Cup Mayonnaise

Directions:

1. You'll need to cook your eggs first by boiling them in salted water they should be hardboiled, so you'll want to cook them for about ten minutes. Place the eggs in a bowl filled with cold water.
2. Peel your eggs and then slice them fine. Do the same to your spring onion, and mix in your diced eggs, sour cream, mayo and

Dijon in a bowl before adding your onion. Leave some onion to garnish with, and then season the bowl with salt and pepper.

3. Scoop out your avocado leaving a half inch to an inch of flesh, and dice your scooped avocado into small pieces.
4. Mix the chopped avocado with your egg mixture.
5. Fill your avocados with the mixture before serving.

Veggie Burgers

Serves: 2

Calories: 637

Fiber: 10.1 Grams

Protein: 23.7 Grams

Fat: 55.1 Grams

Net Carbs: 8.7 Grams

Time: 20 Minutes

Ingredients:

Grilled & Marinated Mushrooms:

- 1 Clove Garlic, Crushed
- Sea Salt & Pepper to Taste
- 1 Tablespoon Ghee
- 2 Portobello Mushrooms, Medium Large
- 1-2 Tablespoons Basil, Chopped & Fresh
- 1 Tablespoon Oregano, Chopped & Fresh

Serve With:

- 2 Eggs, Large
- 2 Tablespoons Mayonnaise
- 2 Keto Buns
- 2 Slices Cheddar Cheese
- 1 Cup Mixed Lettuce

Directions:

1. Start by preparing your mushrooms by seasoning them with garlic, chopped herbs, ghee, salt and pepper. Keep some ghee for frying your eggs. You can cook your mushrooms like this or for added flavor let them marinate for an hour.
2. Put the top sides down on a hot griddle, and then cook for five minutes over medium-high heat. Flip on the other wide, cooking for another five minutes.
3. Remove your mushrooms from heat, and top with cheese slices.
4. Place under the broiler before serving allowing your cheese to melt.
5. While they are broiling fry your eggs with the remainder of your ghee. Cook until the egg is opaque. The yolk should still best lightly runny, and take them off heat.
6. Cut your buns in half, and place the cut side on the hot griddle.
7. Allow your buns to crisp which will take two to three minutes.
8. Assemble your burgers with a tablespoon of mayo on each bun halve and top with your mushrooms. Top with your fried eggs, lettuce and tomato.

Prawn Stir Fry

Serves: 4

Calories: 381

Fiber: 4 Grams

Protein: 21.5 Grams

Fat: 29 Grams

Net Carbs: 8.4 Grams

Time: 20 Minutes

Ingredients:

- 17.6 Ounces Prawns, Peeled & Raw

- 17.6 Ounces Shirataki Noodles, Drained
- 2 Cloves Garlic
- 1 Tablespoon Ginger, Chopped Fine
- 1 Thai Chili Pepper, Small & Seeded
- 1 Tablespoon Coconut Amino
- 3 Tablespoon Fish Sauce
- 2 Cups Bean Sprouts
- ½ Red Pepper, Medium & Deseeded
- 1 Green Pepper, Medium & Deseeded
- ½ Teaspoon Sea Salt, Fine
- 1 ½ Asian Mushrooms, Chopped
- 2 Spring Onions, Medium
- 2 Tablespoons Lime Juice, Fresh
- ½ Cup Ghee
- 1 Bunch Cilantro, Small

Directions:

1. Prepare your noodles as package instructions. Washing and boiling them can help to eliminate odor. Keep in a bowl, setting it to the side once you're done.
2. Halve your chili pepper, removing the seeds. Chop your cilantro stalks. Put the cilantro leaves to the side to use as garnish, and then peel and chop your garlic and ginger. Slice your mushrooms into medium pieces.
3. Grease a pan with half of your ghee, turning the heat to medium-high. Cook your ginger, chili pepper, cilantro stalks and garlic until it becomes fragrant.
4. Add in your prawns, cooking for two to three minutes. Stir to make sure they don't burn.
5. Slice your spring onion, filling it in a bowl of clean water. Take out of the bowl with a slotted spoon, and then drain. Halve and deseed your red and green pepper.
6. Place your onion in a pot that's been greased with the rest of your ghee and cook for another minute. Add in your peppers and mushrooms, continuing to cook for two to three minutes over medium-high heat. It should become tender and crisp.

7. Add in your bean sprouts, cooking for another sixty seconds.
8. Add in your fish sauce, coconut aminos and shirataki noodles. Mix well, cooking for another full minute to heat fully.
9. Add fresh lime juice and garnish with the cilantro leaves before serving.

Easy Chicken Stir Fry

Serves: 4

Calories: 396

Fiber: 3.3 Grams

Protein: 27.6 Grams

Fat: 26.9 Grams

Net Carbs: 7.9 Grams

Time: 20 Minutes

Ingredients:

- 1.1 lbs Chicken Thighs, Boneless & Skinless
- 1 Green Pepper, Medium & Deseeded
- 1 Broccoli, Medium & Stem Removed
- ½ Red Pepper, Medium & Deseeded
- 2 Tablespoons Fish Sauce
- 2 Tablespoon Lime Juice, Fresh
- ½ Teaspoon Sea Salt, Fine
- 1 Red Onion, Medium
- 2 Cloves Garlic
- 1 Thai Chili Pepper, Small & Deseeded
- 1 Tablespoon ginger, Chopped Fine

Directions:

1. Start by cutting your chicken into strips.

2. Net you'll need to prepare your vegetables by peeling and slicing your onion, garlic and ginger.
3. Halve your chili pepper, and then deseed before chopping it fine.
4. Do the same to your red and green peppers, and then cut your broccoli into florets.
5. Set the vegetables to the side and heat two tablespoons of ghee in a large pan.
6. Add your chicken once it's hot, cooking over medium-high heat. The chicken should brown on all sides, and make sure it's completely cooked through.
7. Add ¼ cup more ghee into your pan, adding in your chili pepper, ginger, garlic and onion. Let it cook for two to three minutes. Stir frequently so it doesn't burn, and it should become fragrant in this time.
8. Throw in your green and red pepper, cooking for another two to three minutes before adding your broccoli.
9. Add in your fish sauce, and continue to cook. Your vegetables should be tender and crisp.
10. Add in your lime juice as you take it off of heat.
11. Mix everything together before serving warm.

Spiced Meatballs

Serves: 4

Calories: 447

Fiber: 1.9 Grams

Protein: 27.5 Grams

Fat: 35.4 Grams

Net Carbs: 4.1 Grams

Time: 20 Minutes

Ingredients:

- 0.9 lbs Ground Pork, 20% Fat
- 1 Egg, Large
- ½ Cup Almond Flour
- 1/3 Spanish Chorizo Sausage
- 1 Teaspoon Paprika
- 2 Cloves Garlic
- 1 White Onion, Small
- 1 Tablespoon Ghee
- ¼ Teaspoon Cayenne Pepper
- 1 Teaspoon Ground Cumin
- ½ Teaspoon Sea Salt, Fine

Directions:

1. Dice your onion, garlic and sausage.
2. Grease a pan with ghee, adding in your garlic, chorizo and onion. Cook for five to eight minutes on medium, and it should become crisp. Set it to the side.
3. Take a bowl and combine your egg, ground pork, paprika, cayenne, almond flour, pepper, and ground cumin. Salt the mixture and combine well.
4. Add in your sausage mixture using a slotted spoon so you don't get extra grease in your meat mixture.
5. Make meatballs, placing them on a cutting board.
6. Heat your pan back up, and cook each meatball for two minutes. Turn and cook for another two minutes, reducing heat and cook for another five to ten.
7. Remove from heat and serve warm.

Side Dishes

If you're looking for some sides to add to your speedy entrees, then try out these healthy and delicious ketogenic side recipes. Remember that the salads you use for lunch can double as sides too!

Garlic Broccoli

Serves: 4

Calories: 179

Fiber: 3.9 Grams

Protein: 4.3 Grams

Fat: 14.3 Grams

Net Carbs: 6.9 Grams

Time: 15 Minutes

Ingredients:

- 2 Broccoli, Medium
- ¼ Cup Ghee, Melted
- 2 Tablespoons Lemon Juice, Fresh
- 2-4 Garlic Cloves, Minced
- ½ Teaspoon Sea Salt
- 1 Teaspoon Basil
- ½ Teaspoon Thyme

Directions:

1. Start by heating your oven to 450, and then wash your broccoli before cutting it into florets.
2. Melt your ghee and mix it with your minced garlic.
3. Place your broccoli in a baking dish and cover with your garlic ghee. Drizzle lemon juice over it, and add in your seasoning.
4. Bake for twelve to fifteen minutes.

Summer Salsa

Serves: 4

Calories: 151

Fiber: 1.7 Grams

Protein: 1.4 Grams

Fat: 1.9 Grams

Net Carbs: 4.9 Grams

Time: 10 Minutes

Ingredients:

- 1 Cucumber, Large & Peeled
- ½ Red Onion, Medium
- ¼ Cup Olive Oil
- 2 Tablespoons Parsley, Fresh & Chopped
- Sea Salt & Pepper to Taste
- 1 Tablespoon Lemon Juice, Fresh
- 1 Tablespoon Lime Juice, Fresh
- 2 Cups Cherry Tomatoes, Diced

Directions:

1. Start by dicing your cucumber after peeling it.
2. Dice your onion and chop your tomato finely, and then add in with your cucumber.
3. Mix your lemon juice, lime juice, crushed garlic and olive oil together in a bowl.
4. Pour this mixture over your vegetables.
5. Chop your parsley fine and add it to your vegetables.
6. Season again with salt and pepper to taste.
7. Serve chilled or room temperature.

Guacamole

Serves: 4

Calories: 181

Fiber: 7.8 Grams

Protein: 2.8 Grams

Fat: 14.9 Grams

Net Carbs: 5.4 Grams

Time: 10 Minutes

Ingredients:

- 1 White Onion, Small
- 3 Cloves Garlic, Crushed
- 2 Avocados, Large & Ripe
- 1 1/3 Cup Cherry Tomatoes
- 1 Red Chili Pepper, Small
- 4 Tablespoons Lime Juice, Fresh
- 2-4 Tablespoons Cilantro, Fresh & Chopped
- Sea Salt & Pepper to Taste

Directions:

1. Start by chopping your onion. Halve your chili pepper and deseed it, and then dice your tomato.
2. Halve your avocado, peeling it and removing the seed.
3. Mash your avocado, and then dice your remaining avocado into half inch pieces, putting it to the side.
4. Squeeze your lime juice in, and add in your chopped onion and garlic. Mix well and then add in your chili pepper and tomatoes, mixing again.
5. Add your remaining avocado, salt, pepper and cilantro.

Cheese Sauce

Serves: 4

Calories: 203

Fiber: 0 Grams

Protein: 5.1 Grams

Fat: 20.6 Grams

Net Carbs: 1 Gram

Time: 5 Minutes

Ingredients:

- 2 Tablespoons Butter
- ¼ Cup Heavy Whipping Cream
- ¼ Cup Cream Cheese, Full Fat
- ½ Cup Cheddar, Grated
- 1-2 Tablespoons Water
- Sea Salt to Taste
- ½ Teaspoon Garlic Powder
- ½ Teaspoon Paprika

Directions:

1. Start by putting your butter and cream in a saucepan, heating it up gentle. Grate your cheddar and keep it to the side.
2. Add your cream cheese into the pan once it's heated.
3. Stir until melted, and then as bubbles start to form take it from heat.
4. Add your grated cheddar, and then mix until creamy and smooth. Cook for another three to five minutes if you prefer it thicker. If it does become too thick you can add a little more cream. Stir in your seasoning, and serve warm.

Lemon Green Beans

Serves: 4

Calories: 131

Fiber: 3.7 Grams

Protein: 3.5 Grams

Fat: 9.8 Grams

Net Carbs: 6.5 Grams

Time: 15 Minutes

Ingredients:

- 1 lb Green Beans, Fresh & Trimmed
- ½ Teaspoon Sea Salt
- 2 Tablespoon Olive Oil
- 2 Tablespoon Lemon Juice, Fresh
- 4 Garlic Cloves, Sliced Thin
- 1/3 Cup Almonds, Sliced

Directions:

1. Steam your green beans until tender and crisp.
2. Place in a bowl once steamed, and then add in your lemon juice and salt, tossing to combine.
3. Heat a skillet, greasing with your oil and heating over medium.
4. Add in your almonds, cooking until lightly toasted. Add in your garlic and then let cook for thirty seconds. The garlic should become garlic brown.
5. Add this mixture to your green beans, tossing to combine before serving warm.

Keto Mac & Cheese

Serves: 8

Calories: 294.88

Fiber: 2.71 Grams

Protein: 10.63 Grams

Fat: 25.38 Grams

Net Carbs: 5.47 Grams

Time: 20 Minutes

Ingredients:

- 2 lbs Cauliflower Florets, Frozen
- 4 Ounces Cream Cheese, Cubed
- Sea Salt & Pepper to Taste
- ½ Teaspoon Garlic Powder
- 1 Teaspoon Dijon Mustard
- 8 Ounces Cheddar Cheese, shredded
- 1 Cup Heavy Whipping Cream

Directions:

1. Start by cooking your cauliflower as per package instructions.
2. Simmer your cream in a pan, and whisk to stir the cream cheese in, mixing until smooth.
3. Stir in six ounces of your cheddar cheese. Mix until your cheese melts.
4. Add in your turmeric, garlic, salt, pepper and Dijon mustard. Continue to mix until smooth and well combined.
5. Drain your cauliflower and add your cheese sauce.
6. Top with the remaining cheddar. Stir until melted most of the way.
7. Serve warm.

Asian Broccoli Salad

Serves: 8

Calories: 62

Fiber: 4.72 Grams

Protein: 1.8 Grams

Fat: 4.28 Grams

Net Carbs: 3.62 Grams

Time: 15 Minutes

Ingredients:

- 12 Ounces Broccoli Slaw
- 1 Teaspoon Ginger, Fresh & Grated
- ½ Tablespoon Sesame Seeds
- Cilantro to Garnish
- Sea Salt & Pepper to Taste
- 1 Tablespoon Coconut Aminos
- 2 Tablespoons Coconut Oil
- ½ Cup Goat Milk Yogurt, Full Fat & Plain

Directions:

1. Cook your broccoli slaw covered in a skillet over medium high heat for seven minutes.
2. Uncover and add in your salt, pepper, ginger and coconut aminos. Remove from heat, and add in your yogurt. Top with your sesame seeds.
3. Garnish with cilantro before serving.

Crispy Kale Sprouts

Serves: 2

Calories: 97

Fiber: 1.35 Grams

Protein: 3.89 Grams

Fat: 8.45 Grams

Net Carbs: 0.82 Grams

Time: 15 Minutes

Ingredients:

- 4 Ounces Kale Sprouts
- 2 Tablespoon Parmesan Cheese
- Sea Salt & Pepper to Taste
- Oil for Frying

Directions:

1. Stat by preparing your deep fryer, making sure it's hot and you have clean oil for frying.
2. Make a single layer of kale sprout sin your fryer basket, and then fry until they start to brown around the edges.
3. Drain excess grease, and repeat for remaining kale.
4. Serve warm.

Sugar Snap Peas with Bacon

Serves: 3

Calories: 147.33

Fiber: 1.77 Grams

Protein: 1.95 Grams

Fats: 13.04 Grams

Net Carbs: 4.33 Grams

Time: 15 Minutes

Ingredients:

- ½ Teaspoon Red Pepper Flakes
- 3 Tablespoons Bacon Fat, Rendered

- ½ Large Lemon, Juiced
- 3 Cups Sugar Snap Peas
- 2 Teaspoons Garlic, Minced

Directions:

1. Add three tablespoons of bacon fat in a pan bringing it to its smoking point.
2. Add two teaspoons of garlic and reduce the heat to medium. Cook until fragrant and browned lightly, which should take one to two minutes.
3. Add in your sugar snap peas, and let cook for another two to three minutes.
4. Add your lemon juice, stirring well and cooing for one to two more minutes.
5. Take off of heat and garnish with red pepper flakes and lemon zest if desired, serving warm.

Red Pepper Spinach Salad

Serves: 2

Calories: 212.86

Fiber: 2.37 Grams

Protein: 6.5 Grams

Fat: 19.49 Grams

Net Carbs: 2.64 Grams

Time: 10 Minutes

Ingredients:

- 6 Cups Spinach, Fresh
- 1 Teaspoon Red Pepper Flakes
- 3 Tablespoons Parmesan Cheese, Grated
- ¼ Cup Keto Ranch Dressing

Directions:

1. Add your ranch dressing, mixing with your spinach. Add in your red pepper flakes, mixing well.
2. Top with parmesan cheese and serve.

Snack Recipes

Your meal plan won't take up your full twenty net carbs a day, so you'll need to add in snacks or dessert to fill your net carb allowance. By eating all of the net carbs you need, you shouldn't be hungry which is one of the benefits of the ketogenic diet.

Fried Cheese

Serves: 2

Calories: 515

Fiber: 4.1 Grams

Protein: 24.5 Grams

Fat: 43.3 Grams

Net Carbs: 4.5 Grams

Time: 10 Minutes

Ingredients:

- 3 Tablespoons Flax meal
- 5.3 Ounces Halloumi Cheese or Kefalotyri
- Ghee for Frying
- 3 Tablespoons Almond Flour, Heaping

Directions:

1. Start by cutting your cheese into half inch slices.
2. Pour some cold water into a bowl and set the bowl aside.
3. Take another bowl and mix together your flax meal and almond flour.
4. Dip each cheese slice into your cold water and then into your almond flour mixture.
5. Make sure all of your sides are covered, and then shake off any excess breading. Set aside until all of your cheese is covered.

6. Heat a heavy bottomed pan using your ghee, and once your oil is hot start adding in your cheese slices.
7. Fry for about two minutes on each side. Both sides should be crisp and golden.

Pesto Bombs

Serves: 8

Calories: 123

Fiber: 0.3 Grams

Protein: 4.3 Grams

Fat: 12.9 Grams

Net Carbs: 1.3 Grams

Time: 5 Minutes

Ingredients:

- 1 Cup Cream Cheese, Full Fat
- 2 Tablespoons Basil Pesto
- ½ Cup Parmesan Cheese, Grated
- 10 Olives, Sliced

Directions:

1. Mix all of your ingredients together besides your cucumber.
2. Slice your cucumber, and use the cucumbers as chips to dip into the dip.

Cheesecake Dip

Serves: 4

Calories: 195

Fiber: 0.3 Grams

Protein: 7.9 Grams

Fat: 18.3 Grams

Net Carbs: 3 Grams

Time: 5 Minutes

Ingredients:

- 1 Cup Sour Cream, Full Fat
- 5-10 Drops Stevia Extract
- 2 Tablespoons Swerve
- ¼ Cup Vanilla Protein Powder
- ½ Cup Cream Cheese, Full Fat
- 1 Vanilla Bean

Directions:

1. Cut your vanilla bean lengthwise, scraping out the seeds carefully.
2. Mix all ingredients together and serve with fresh berries. It'll keep in the fridge for three days.

Zucchini Rolls

Serves: 4

Calories: 257

Fiber: 1.3 Grams

Protein: 15.7 Grams

Fat: 19.2 Grams

Net Carbs: 5 Grams

Time: 20 Minutes

Ingredients:

- 3 Baby Zucchini (or Small Zucchini)
- 1 Cup Goat Cheese, Soft
- 14 Slices Streaky Bacon, Thin
- ½ Cup Sun Dried Tomatoes, Drained
- 4 Tablespoons Raspberry Vinegar
- ½ Cup Basil, Fresh

Directions:

1. Start by turning your oven to 400.
2. Slice lengthwise in thin strips.
3. Put your vinegar in a bowl, and place your zucchini in it, covering for ten minutes.
4. Cut your bacon lengthwise, and place it on a baking tray that's been lined with parchment paper.
5. Bake until crisp, which will take about five minutes. However, it should still be soft enough to roll.
6. Put your zucchini down and add your bacon strip on top. Top with sundried tomatoes, basil and goat cheese.
7. Roll up and serve.

Easy Parmesan Crisps

Serves: 4

Calories: 233

Fiber: 1.9 Grams

Protein: 19.6 Grams

Fat: 14.5 Grams

Net Carbs: 2.7 Grams

Time: 15-20 Minutes

Ingredients:

- 4 Tablespoons Coconut Flour

- 7.1 Ounces Parmesan Cheese, Grated
- 2 Teaspoons Rosemary

Directions:

1. Start by turning your oven to 350.
2. Mix your coconut flour and parmesan cheese in a bowl. Do not use powdery parmesan. You need one that is in small chunks. Add in your rosemary, mixing well.
3. Scoop a teaspoon of the mixture, and place it on the baking try that's been lined with parchment paper. Leave a gap between each, repeating until your mixture has been used.
4. Bake for ten to fifteen minutes. They should turn golden brown, and then let cool before serving.

Garlic Fried Zucchini

Serves: 6

Calories: 233

Fiber: 2.2 Grams

Protein: 14.3 Grams

Fat: 16.7 Grams

Net Carbs: 4.3 Grams

Time: 20 Minutes

Ingredients:

Zucchini Chips:

- 2 Zucchini, Medium & Sliced in ½ Inch Rounds
- 2 Eggs, Large
- 1 ½ Cups Parmesan Cheese, Grated
- 4 Tablespoons Coconut Flour, Heaping
- ½ Teaspoon Italian Seasoning
- ½ Teaspoon Paprika

- 6 Tablespoons Coconut Oil
- ½ Teaspoon Sea Salt, Fine
- ½ Teaspoon Garlic Powder

Dipping Sauce:

- ½ Teaspoon Pepper
- ½ Teaspoon Garlic Salt
- 2 Tablespoons Fresh Dill, Minced
- ½ Cup Plain Yogurt, Full Fat
- 1 Tablespoon Lemon Juice, Fresh

Directions:

1. Start by slicing your zucchini, and then arrange three bowls.
2. Whisk your eggs in one, add your parmesan in another, and then add your coconut flour in the last bowl. Mix your spices with your coconut flour.
3. Heat your coconut oil in a skillet using medium-high heat. Dip your zucchini into each bowl. Start with your coconut flour, then your egg, and then dip in your parmesan.
4. Fry in the skillet for one to two minutes on each side.
5. Drain on a paper towel, letting cool.
6. Mix all of your dipping ingredients together, and serve with your zucchini chips.

Dessert Recipes

Snacks and desserts are important for your keto diet, since you should take in 20 net carbs every day to keep from being hungry. While most people will choose two snacks. Here are some desserts that can help to satisfy your sweet tooth and fill out your net carb allowance every day. Most people on a ketogenic diet will eat two snacks daily.

Brownie Mug Cake

Serves: 2

Calories: 397

Fiber: 7.5 Grams

Protein: 8 Grams

Fat: 38.3 Grams

Net Carbs: 6.9 Grams

Time: 10 Minutes

Ingredients:

- 2 Squares Dark Chocolate, Large & Grated
- ¼ Cup Cacao Powder, Unsweetened
- ½ Teaspoon Cinnamon
- 2 Tablespoons Chia Seeds, Ground
- 1 Teaspoon Baking Powder
- ¼ Cup Coconut Oil, Melted
- 1 Egg, Large
- ¼ Cup Coffee, Freshly Brewed
- 4 Tablespoon Swerve
- Pinch Sea Salt

Directions:

1. Combine all of your dry ingredients together.

2. Add in your coconut oil, coffee, and egg before mixing well. Mix swerve.
3. Divide between two mugs, and then microwave for seventy to ninety seconds. It should be cooked all the way through.

Cinnamon Mug Cake

Serves: 1

Calories: 333

Fiber: 4.4 Grams

Protein: 11.8 Grams

Fat: 28.6 Grams

Net Carbs: 3.9 Grams

Time: 5 Minutes

Ingredients:

- 1 Tablespoon Coconut Flour, Heaping
- 2 Tablespoons Almond Flour, Heaping
- 1/8 Teaspoon Baking Soda
- ½ Teaspoon Ground Cinnamon
- 1 Tablespoon Swerve
- 1 Egg, Large
- 1 Tablespoon Coconut Oil

Directions:

1. Mix all of your dry ingredients together, combining thoroughly.
2. Add in your coconut oil and egg, mixing well.
3. Microwave on high for seventy to ninety seconds until cooked through entirely.

Chocolate Frostino

Serves: 2

Calories: 421

Fiber: 4.3 Grams

Protein: 16.3 Gams

Fat: 36.8 Grams

Net Carbs: 6 Grams

Time: 5 Minutes

Ingredients:

- 1 Cup Coconut Milk
- 2 Tablespoon Cacao Powder
- 2 Cups Ice
- 2 Scoops Collagen, Keto Friendly
- 1 Tablespoon Almond Butter, Heaped

Directions:

1. Start by placing everything in a blender, blending until smooth.
2. Pour into serving glasses and enjoy!

Pumpkin Spice Latte

Serves: 2

Calories: 353

Fiber: 1.1 Grams

Protein: 2.8 Grams

Fat: 37.8 Grams

Net Carbs: 4.9 Grams

Time: 5 Minutes

Ingredients:

- 1 Cup Coffee, Freshly Brewed
- ¼ Teaspoon Vanilla Bean Powder
- ½ Teaspoon Pumpkin Pie Spice
- ¼ Cup Pumpkin Puree
- 1 Cup Coconut Milk, Unsweetened
- ¼ Teaspoon Turmeric Powder
- 1/8 Teaspoon Black Pepper
- 2 Tablespoons MCT Oil

Directions:

1. Heat up your coconut milk in a small saucepan, cooking until bubbles start to appear.
2. Place all other ingredients in a blender, blending well.
3. Add in your coconut milk and blend again.

Turmeric Iced Latte

Serves: 8

Calories: 247

Fiber: 0.8 Grams

Protein: 3 Grams

Fat: 25.6 Grams

Net Carbs: 4.4 Grams

Time: 10 Minutes

Ingredients:

- 2 Cups Coconut Milk, Unsweetened
- 1 Tablespoon Ginger, Grated Fresh
- 1 Teaspoon Cinnamon

- 2 Cups Almond Milk, Unsweetened
- 2 Tablespoons Turmeric, Grated Fresh
- 1 Teaspoon Vanilla Powder
- ¼ Teaspoon Pepper

Directions:

1. Place your almond milk and coconut n a pan, and then add in your vanilla, ginger, turmeric and pepper.
2. Bring to a boil, simmering for five minutes.
3. Strain through a cheese cloth, and then blend until fully combined.
4. Allow to cool and then pour over ice to serve.

Chocolate Chip Cookies

Serves: 2

Calories: 381

Fiber: 6.3 Grams

Protein: 10.7 Grams

Fat: 29.6 Grams

Net Carbs: 6.2 Grams

Time: 5 Minutes

Ingredients:

- 1 Egg Yolk, Large
- 1/3 Cup Toasted Almond Butter
- 2 Tablespoons Dark Chocolate, Chopped
- Pinch Sea Salt
- 2 Tablespoons Swerve

Directions:

1. Mix your egg yolk, swerve, salt, and almond butter.

2. Add in your dark chocolate, mixing well.
3. Divide your dough between ramekins, and then microwave for sixty to ninety seconds. Check halfway to make sure it doesn't burn. The longer you leave them in there, the crispier the cookies will become.

Mint & Chocolate Smoothie

Serves: 1

Calories: 401

Fiber: 7.8 Grams

Protein: 5 Grams

Fat: 40.3 Grams

Net Carbs: 6.5 Grams

Time: 5 Minutes

Ingredients:

- ½ Avocado, Medium
- ¼ Cup Coconut Milk
- 1 Cup Almond Milk, Unsweetened
- 2 Tablespoons Swerve
- 1 Tablespoon MCT Oil
- 2-3 Ice Cubes
- 1 Tablespoon Cocoa Powder, Unsweetened
- 2-4 Mint Leaves

Directions:

1. Blend all ingredients together in a blender.
2. Serve immediately.

Hot Spiced Mocha

Serves: 2

Calories: 302

Fiber: 2.2 Grams

Protein: 3.6 Grams

Fat: 31.7 Grams

Net Carbs: 5.4 Grams

Time: 10 Minutes

Ingredients:

- 1 Tablespoon Coconut Oil
- ¼ Teaspoon Vanilla Bean Powder
- Pinch Cayenne Pepper
- ¼ Teaspoon Ground Cardamom
- 1 Cup Coconut Milk, Unsweetened
- 2 Tablespoon Raw Cacao Powder, Unsweetened
- ½ Teaspoon Cinnamon
- 2 Tablespoons Swerve
- 1 ½ Cup Coffee, Freshly Brewed

Directions:

1. Pour your coconut milk into a small pan, mixing in your cocoa powder. Add in your swerve, vanilla, cinnamon, cardamom, and cayenne pepper. Bring the mixture to a simmer, cooking for a minute before taking it off of heat.
2. Add in your coconut oil and coffee, whisking well.
3. Enjoy warm.

Chocolate Mug

Serves: 4

Calories: 337

Fiber: 14.3 Grams

Protein: 6 Grams

Fat: 31.4 Grams

Net Carbs: 6.9 Grams

Time: 15 Minutes

Ingredients:

Chocolate Filling:

- 1 Teaspoon Vanilla Powder
- 2 ½ Avocados, Large & Peeled & Deseeded
- ½ Cup Cacao Powder, Raw
- 2 Tablespoons Coconut Oil
- Pinch Sea Salt
- 1-2 Tablespoons Almond Milk, Unsweetened
- ¾ Teaspoon Liquid Stevia

Chocolate Curls:

- 15 Grams Cocoa Butter
- 2/3 Teaspoon Liquid Stevia
- 1/3 Cup Cocoa Powder, Raw

Directions:

1. Place all of your chocolate filling ingredients in a bowl, blending with a hand blender until smooth.
2. Spoon into four different ramekins.
3. Place your cocoa butter in a double boiler, and then melt over medium heat. Remove from heat before stirring in swerve.
4. Allow to cool slightly, and then spread on a marble board. It should still be tacky but mostly set. Use a scraper to make flakes or curls.
5. Enjoy immediately.

Berry Sauce & Pancake

Berry Sauce Serving: 4

Pancake Serving: 1

Calories: 347

Fiber: 5 Grams

Protein: 22.4 Grams

Fat: 22.4 Grams

Net Carbs: 6.6 Grams

Time: 15 Minutes

Ingredients:

Berry Sauce:

- ½ Cup Wild Blueberries, Fresh
- ½ Cup Blackberries, Fresh
- 2 Tablespoons Swerve
- 3 Tablespoons Water
- ¼ Teaspoon Vanilla Powder
- 2 Teaspoons Chia Seeds, Ground
- 1 Tablespoon Lemon Juice, Fresh

Pancake:

- ½ Teaspoon Lemon Zest, Fresh
- 2 Tablespoons Coconut Flour
- 1 Teaspoon Ghee
- 2 Tablespoons Swerve
- 3 Eggs, Large
- ¼ Teaspoon Cream of Tartar

Directions:

1. You need to start preparing your berry sauce first. Put your blueberries and blackberries in a saucepan adding in your vanilla

powder, lemon juice, swerve and water. Turn it up to medium heat, and cook until your berries soften. Take off of heat, mixing in your chia seeds.

2. Let it stand for ten to fifteen minutes until thickened.
3. Now you can start to prepare your pancake, setting the oven to 400.
4. Separate your egg yolk from your egg whites, and then mix the egg yolks with a fork.
5. Start by beating your egg whites using medium-low heat, beating for about two minutes until they start to become foamy.
6. Add in your cream of tartar, and then add in your swerve one tablespoon at a time. Continue to beat until soft peaks first.
7. Add in your lemon zest and then your egg yolks, folding them in with a spatula.
8. Sift your coconut flour in, mixing slowly to combine. Make sure you don't deflate your egg whites.
9. Spread your pancake batter in a skillet that's heated and prepared with ghee. Turn the heat to low, cooking for five minutes. The bottom of your pancake should brown, and then remove from the burner. Place in your oven to broil for three to five minutes or until the top browns lightly.
10. Serve with your berry sauce on top, and reserve the rest of the berry sauce in an airtight container in the fridge for up to a week.

Red Velvet Mug

Serves: 2

Calories: 565

Fiber: 4.2 Grams

Protein: 14.7 Grams

Fat: 54 Grams

Net Carbs: 8 Grams

Time: 10 Minutes

Ingredients:

Cake:

- 1 Tablespoon Coconut Flour, Heaping
- 1 Tablespoon Cocoa Powder, Unsweetened
- 1/3 Cup Almond Flour
- ¼ Teaspoon Baking Soda
- 1 Tablespoon Beetroot Powder
- 2 Eggs, Large
- 3 Tablespoons Swerve
- ¼ Teaspoon Vanilla Powder
- ¼ Cup Sour Cream, Full Fat
- 2 Tablespoons Coconut Oil
- 2-3 Drops Red Food Coloring, Natural

Frosting:

- 2 Tablespoons Butter, Room Temperature
- 1 Tablespoon Swerve
- ¼ Teaspoon Vanilla Powder
- ¼ Cup Cream Cheese, Full Fat

Directions:

1. Place your cacao powder, coconut flour, almond flour, baking soda, beetroot powder, swerve, and vanilla powder in a bowl, mixing well.
2. Add in your melted coconut oil, sour cream, and eggs, mixing well.
3. Divide the mix between two mugs, and then microwave each one for seventy to ninety seconds.
4. Start to prepare your frosting by mixing your swerve, cream cheese, vanilla and butter together. Blend until you reach a smooth texture.
5. Let your cakes cool before applying your frosting. Serve cooled.

Eggnog Mug Cake

Serves: 1

Calories: 339

Fiber: 4.1 Grams

Protein: 11.8 Grams

Fat: 28.7 Grams

Net Carbs: 4.4 Grams

Time: 5 Minutes

Ingredients:

- 2 Tablespoons Almond Flour, Heaping
- ¼ Teaspoon Ground Cinnamon
- 1/8 Teaspoon Ground Nutmeg
- 1 Tablespoon Coconut Flour, Heaping
- 2 Tablespoons Swerve
- 1/8 Teaspoon Baking Soda
- 1 Egg, Large
- ½ Teaspoon Rum Extract
- 1 Tablespoon Coconut Oil

Directions:

1. Mix all dry ingredients together.
2. Add in your swerve, egg, coconut oil, and rum extract, mixing well.
3. Microwave for seventy to ninety seconds and serve once cooled.

Strawberry Milkshake

Serves: 1

Calories: 275

Fiber: 2 Grams

Protein: 2.5 Grams

Fat: 27.4 Grams

Net Carbs: 6.4 Grams

Time: 5 Minutes

Ingredients:

- 1 Tablespoon MCT Oil
- ½ Cup Strawberries, Fresh
- ¼ Cup Coconut Milk, Unsweetened
- ¾ Cup Almond Milk, Unsweetened
- ½ Teaspoon Vanilla Extract, Sugar Free
- 4-6 Ice Cubes

Directions:

1. Blend all ingredients together and then serve.

Vanilla Mug Cake

Serves: 1

Calories: 334

Fiber: 3.7 Grams

Protein: 11.8 Grams

Fat: 28.6 Grams

Net Carbs: 4.2 Grams

Time: 5 Minutes

Ingredients:

- 2 Tablespoons Swerve
- 1/8 Teaspoon Baking Soda

- ¼ Teaspoon Vanilla Bean Powder
- 2 Tablespoons Almond Flour, Heaping
- 1 Tablespoon Coconut Flour, Heaping
- 1 Egg, Large
- 1 Tablespoon Coconut Oil

Directions:

1. Combine all dry ingredients together in a mug.
2. Add in your swerve, coconut oil and egg, mixing well with a fork.
3. Microwave for seventy to ninety seconds.
4. Let cool before serving.

Orange Chocolate Chia Pudding

Serves: 1

Calories: 357

Fiber: 12.4 Grams

Protein: 9.2 Grams

Fat: 29.2 Grams

Net Carbs: 6.9 Grams

Time: 15 Minutes

Ingredients:

- ½ Cup Water
- ¼ Cup Coconut Milk, Unsweetened
- ¼ Cup Chia Seeds
- 1 Tablespoon Swerve
- ½ Teaspoon Orange Zest, Fresh
- 5-10 Drops Stevia Extract
- 2 Tablespoons Dark Chocolate, 85%

Directions:

1. Mix your water, swerve, chia seeds, and coconut together. If you want a smooth texture grind your chia seeds beforehand.
2. Add in your orange zest, stevia, and then mix. Let it stand for ten to fifteen minutes before serving top with dark chocolate chips.

Conclusion

Now you know everything you need to in order to start your ketogenic diet today. You don't need tons of time in order to start your keto diet today. With this diet and moderate exercise, you'll stay in shape, stay healthy and lose the weight you want! Remember that you can modify your meal plan or create one for yourself. It's important to enjoy your food if you plan to stick to a diet, and the ketogenic diet is customizable and delicious! There's no reason to keep from reaching your diet goals and start your journey to a healthier and happier you today.

Lastly, if you have enjoyed the book, can your please leave a review for me on Amazon? I really would appreciate it! -Sydney Foster.

EXTRA Bonus! Subscribe to the free newsletter for free recipes, articles and more at: www.KetoDiet.Coach

92645621R00061

Made in the USA
Columbia, SC
29 March 2018